21 DAY DEVOTIONAL

a Woman's Devotional to Unveiling Her Mask
and Live Life Unapologetically On Purpose

LA TANYA D. WALKER

Foreword by Dr. Connie Stewart

CONFIDENTIAL CONVERSATIONS™
21 DAY DEVOTIONAL

a Woman's Devotional to Unveiling Her Mask
and Live Life Unapologetically On Purpose

byDə'zīne Publishing

Houston, Texas

Editor: Sharon C. Jenkins
Cover Photo: HR Designz

ISBN:978-0-692-72293-0

For more information about books written and by La Tanya D. Walker, or special discounts for bulk purchases, please visit www.latanyadwalker.com or write to:

La Tanya D. Walker International
c/o byDə'zīne Publishing
P.O. Box 31038
Houston, Texas 77231
Printed in the United States of America

This book is dedicated to

Tempestt Bre'elle and Noelle Denise.

No matter what life throws at you, remember there's nothing you can't do when God's involved.

~Me

Be Bold. Be Brilliant. Be Beautiful.
Be...Authentically You!™

~La Tanya D. Walker

Table of Contents

Foreword

WE, AS WOMEN HAVE FOUGHT LONG AND hard to find and take our place in the world. We are movers and shakers, coaches and cheerleaders and so much more! You know, I'm "every" woman...it's all in me. While there is nothing wrong with that, it makes it hard for us to be honest when things go wrong. Yes, believe it or not things do go wrong! However, the hardest part about being everything to everyone is that we have trouble being honest with ourselves.

Author, La Tanya D. Walker gives us that chance in Confidential Conversations™. Often times when the bottom falls out, our immediate reaction is to fix IT and not US! Walker allowed her pain to not only help her, but so many others. This 21-day devotional allows you to take off the cape and deal with the real you. Not who you are to everyone else, but who you are in Him.

It speaks of issues we all go through but aren't always willing to talk about. Sometimes we need an invitation to remove the mask. Being real with ourselves is not always easy. Sometimes God has to break our will in order to get our attention. When we realize there is nothing we can do in our own power we give ourselves permission to be weak so His strength can be made perfect in us. Coach Walker assures us that it is in that place when we exchange our break down for a break through!

La Tanya invites us to journey with her in hopes that we are able to see ourselves without our mask and have some life changing confidential conversations. If we embrace the principles she has laid out for us this devotional is sure to inspire, empower and encourage us all.

Let the conversations begin!

Dr. Connie Stewart

Life Coach, *Life in Bloom Life Coach Institute of Bloom University*

Senior Pastor, *Believer's Empowerment Church*

Author's Notes

Dear Reader,

THANK YOU FOR BUYING AND READING MY FIRST book. I pray this is only the beginning of our sisterhood and a long reading relationship.

I'll be the first to admit that I don't have all the answers and so that we are clear, this book is not one where I will tell you I've found the fix. In fact, it's just the opposite. It is a collection of the past 20 months of personal and business failures, live Internet broadcasts, teleconferences, preached sermons and motivational speaking in written word during my personal quest to "fix me." It's the past 20 months of how God took what was completely broken in me and is using it to empower, restore and transform not only the lives of women around the world, but yours truly.

Not too long ago I read while doing research for one of my Confidential Conversations™ Women's Empowerment Seminars that you teach what you need to learn, so this book is about those things I needed to learn. The things I, after doing a little soul searching realized I couldn't do by myself any longer – that I needed God's help to fix. So here I am through 21 unique conversations, my personal devotional, unveiling my masks and revealing things I needed and am still learning in an effort to become the woman God created.

You should know that this is not, nor will it ever be a one-size fit all devotional. You know the ones that give you a topic, suggest a prayer and ask you to journal about that day's topic. No, this is a devotional that discloses my hurts, pains, and triumphs; with hopes that you can put yourself in my shoes from time to time and get honest with yourself about the hurts you've experienced or are experiencing and give them to God to fix. And while the experts say that it requires a minimum of 21 days of doing the same thing over and over before it becomes a habit, your journey to reach the wholeness God has for you will never resemble mine or that of another sister reading this book. As a matter of fact, because some of you have had your masks on for what seems like a lifetime, your journey will start and stop with your willingness to fully submit and yield to God's will.

What Confidential Conversations™ is has nothing to do with a few secrets that may be disclosed here in the book or what you even chose to say to yourself as you read along. Yet it does have to do with what you choose not to disclose or should I say, the things hiding behind your mask. The things you're keeping secret and those things that are keeping you from total surrender. As I mentioned before, Confidential Conversations™, was about my personal journey to fix me. The woman who on the surface appeared to always have it together, but when you pulled back the layers you found that she harbored a fear of failure, a fear of success, abuse, a need for acceptance and skirting the lines of depression. It is about the entrepreneur, the mother, the professional woman or the young lady who knows she has what it takes to reach the level she has potential to achieve but, because things from her past haunt her, she can't seem to get there. It's about the woman who is continuously missing the mark because she can't seem to get it together and if she does, she can't seem to keep it together because she's broken. And last, but not least, Confidential Conversations™ is about the woman reading this book, who may also be experiencing similar if not the same issues and want to stop hiding behind the mask that keeps the world from seeing her imperfections and become completely whole again.

If you were one of the women who faithfully tuned in on a weekly teleconference, a live Internet broadcast via Periscope, Facebook or attended a Confidential Conversations™ women's empowerment seminar, thank you for inspiring me to go deeper to become my authentic self. My prayer is that long after you've read the book, you will continue to benefit from the 21 conversations. After reading, I'd love to hear how my life's lessons helped you on your journey to becoming authentically you, and if you'd like, you are more than welcome to share your story about how they transformed your life at info@confidentialconversations.org.

The Confidential Conversations™ platform was my gift from God and to repay him, a significant portion of my royalties from this book will be used to support Confidential Conversations™ Women's Empowerment Network, Inc. ("Confidential Conversations™ W.E.N.") Confidential Conversations™ W.E.N., is a nonprofit organization seeking its 501c3 status to provide programs and services that support the whole woman, including but not limited to: the Authentically You™ Women's Retreat, Confidential Conversations™ Real Talk w/Real Women Power Luncheons and

Confidential Conversations™ at Home. Through this unique blend of ministry and outreach, women across the country can expect their lives to be enriched spiritually, professionally and financially.

To learn more about Confidential Conversations™, see www.confidentialconversations.org and while you're there, check out our upcoming events in a city near you.

Thank you again for sharing this journey with me and being willing to unveil your mask and start anew. I pray you enjoy it.

Your sister and friend,

~La Tanya D. Walker
www.latanyadwalker.com

Before We Begin

YOUR JOURNEY IS A PERSONAL ONE, SO TIME spent at Jesus' feet is important. As you embark on your personal 21-day journey to unveil your mask, approach each day prayer. Ask God to allow you to see things as they really are, then accept and fall in love with the things you cannot change about you. It is my prayer that through my experiences, good and bad, professional and personal; women across the country will begin serious dialogues and get down to the grit of their insecurities and allow God to fix us. You may find yourself laughing or even crying at times, and that's okay, because what matters most is you are getting to a place where you are real with yourself. So real, that you are busting through the glass ceiling of opposition and on your way to living life unapologetically on purpose.

I've included with each day an area called Unveil the Mask, where I've added Scripture for you to meditate on. During your time of meditation, ask the Lord to show himself in his word and to show you who you really are, so that you can start to remove your mask. When you take off your mask, you will solidify your "born again" experience by becoming equipped and empowered to walk in your responsibility to become all that God created you to be. To help you prepare, I've listed five Scriptures you may want to use as a point of reference before you begin.

- *"But you, when you pray, go into your room, and when you have shut your door, pray to your Father who is in the secret place; and your Father, who sees in secret will reward you openly. And when you pray, do not use vain repetitions as the heathen do. For they think they will be heard for their many words. Therefore, do not be like them. For your Father knows the things you have need of before you ask Him." ~Matthew 6:8 (NKJV)* Jesus, in the book of Matthew sets the ultimate example by teaching us how to pray. Each day before you begin, go into your secret place and pray.

- *"My sheep hear My voice, and I know them, and they follow me." ~John 10:27 (KJV)* Pray that you may be able to position yourself to clearly hear God's voice over the next 21 days. That may require getting alone. When is it that you feel you're most open to receiving from Him. I've found that I hear Him best in the early hours of the morning, so I meet with God at 5:30 a.m., daily. Set a time and date to meet with Him and let that be your time where you are positioned to hear.

- *"...it is Christ who died and furthermore is also risen, who is even at the right hand of God, who also makes intercession for us."* ~ *Romans 8:34b (NKJV)* Pray for others as Holy Spirit intercedes for you. Because He already knows us and the desires of our hearts, spend time throughout the next 21 days praying for those you love, your church, community leaders, or a person in need. As you pray for them, watch how God begin to release his supernatural powers and bless you in the areas you need most.

- *"But those who wait on the Lord shall renew their strength; they shall mount up with wings like eagles, they shall run and not be weary, they shall walk and not faint."* ~*Isaiah 40:31 (NKJV)*. When you begin to remove your masks, the old you is going to be in direct competition opposing the new you. Don't faint. Pray for strength that only comes from time spent with the Lord.

▪   *"Finally my brethren, be strong in the Lord and in the power of His might. Put on the whole armor of God that you may be able to stand against the wiles of the devil."* *~Ephesians 6:10-11 (NKJV).*   Ridding yourself of the hurts and pains you've endured over the years not only takes time, but it is outright hard! Everything and everybody will try and come against you in your quest to be better. Remember, you are not fighting the person, it's a spiritual warfare. One that will try and come against you with every trick in the book. That's why it is an absolute must to pray against the spirit of darkness!

CHAPTER ONE

Bruised but Not Broken

C AN I BE HONEST WITH YOU? IT WAS NOT LONG ago that I saw myself like the world saw brokenness; ugly, unwanted and useless. That was until I totally surrendered my all and decided I could no longer do life on my own. No, I didn't contemplate suicide, at least not this time. Instead, I began to completely lean and depend on the power of God in every aspect of my life because I tried doing things my way and as you can imagine it didn't work out. For years I claimed to be a 'faith walker,' but I was a hypocrite. The words I spoke and the things I said about myself to myself and others didn't seem to line up with what my heart truly felt, and I began to sink.

I remember it like it was yesterday. It was a gorgeous fall morning, and there I was sitting upstairs in the office of my one-bedroom loft apartment reviewing a forecasted budget for the upcoming fiscal year 2015 and the phone rings. I laugh as I write this because no sooner than I said hello, the person on the other end of the phone gave me the news that began a true test of my authenticity. It was news that due to the downturn in oil and gas, they were cutting thirty percent of their workforce and would no longer require the services my company provided. Call me crazy because I think all of my clients had gotten together and conspired against me. Not one, but all of them called over the course of the next few weeks with the same story.

Unlike most people, fear really didn't hit me, at least not then because a few months prior I had stopped running and accepted my call into Ministry. I knew the moment I said, "yes," the enemy was going to be hard pressed after me, so I had an idea that I was probably being 'considered.' However, as we moved into 2015 and one, two, three months passed without a penny of revenue generated in my business, fear began to sink in, and I got a severe case of the "what if's?" What if I can't bounce back and do this again? What if this time I lose everything? What if I get evicted? What if I lose my car? My business? For the first time in as long as I can remember in my career as an entrepreneur, I was literally horrified.

I remember calling an old business partner in Atlanta and sharing my story with her. I told her my dilemma and her response was, "Girl quit tripping, you are the Queen of Reinvention, the Olivia Pope of Small Business. If anyone can fix this, it's you." And she was right, for years if things weren't going the way I thought they should in my business or personal life, I would quickly assess the situation and make the necessary changes even if those changes meant packing up and starting over. I called it 'reinvention,' not realizing I was masking the real problem.   God wasn't included. Of course, I would pray and asked God to bless me and my business, but I hadn't involved Him in the recovery process. I hadn't committed my business to Him.

Here I was going on year 15 as an entrepreneur, having received numerous awards and recognitions for my success in business, but my life was in shambles. God was sitting me down for what I found later to serve a greater purpose. I could not for the life of me get it together. I was spiraling down with no visibility of a safety net around to save me. I was broken, and I mean bad, so as I started on my personal journey to fix me or reinvent me, this time, unlike all the others I couldn't make it click. Things weren't jiving. I lost my creativity, my mojo was stale, and me, the Queen of Reinvention - the Olivia Pope of small business had hit rock bottom emotionally. The girl who had just been honored for her successes in business, the girl whose business was just short of making its first million, the one who mentored other aspiring business owners couldn't take it anymore. She just couldn't seem to bust through the glass ceiling like many of her counterparts and in my transparency, I had fallen hard. I lost everything; the place where I laid my head, my car, the respect of my family and friends and months later my business. And like many of you reading, I too, needed to put on a mask, because if nothing else, "I was never supposed to let 'em see me sweat, right?"

Over the course of a few weeks from the time I'd spoken with my friend, I started to list all of the things I thought were keeping me from moving forward. As it turned out I listed seven reasons for the failure in my life and my business, so I prayed about them and later found myself conducting a short survey of a few women, of which 8 out of 10 that were surveyed felt just like me. They could not move forward for various reasons and what I soon realized is we all shared a common bond. From difficulty in our homes, with our credit or finances, troubled relationships, our education or a lack there of, living in what some considered the dreadful single life or the one I came to most recently know; and that was not knowing what God purposed me to do. We were broken, and because the world looks at what is broken as ugly or useless, we all put on our masks. Here I am with secrets of those who shared, I asked God, "Now that I know what I know, what is it you want me to do with it?" Hence the birth of Confidential Conversations™

A few months later in my Ministers Development Class at The Fountain of Praise Church in Houston, Texas, I was tasked to prepare my first sermon based on one of two topics; healing or sin. As I contemplated my own brokenness and all I'd gone through the past several months, I chose healing. From my not fully trusting God would do what he said he'd do and involving someone in my business who I later found out was nothing short of a professional con artist to the client I thought I could trust, yet they stole from me. I wanted to tell my classmates, other ministers, about the interviews I went on where some of the people included were friends and how they'd praised me publicly, but stabbed me in the back privately. I wanted to tell them how I was bruised, but not broken as a testimony of God's goodness and how he enabled me to overcome.

You recall earlier I told you I had jotted down seven things I thought were stopping me? I didn't realize it then, but weeks later the Holy Spirit spoke to me and said, "seven because it represents completion, and it will be through those things that I will begin to restore and make you whole again. While you want to tell them how you were bruised, but not broken - how they hurt you, but you're still standing, I want you to tell them about the blessings behind brokenness." As you continue reading, I want you to know that there are blessings behind the brokenness, but you can't get there if you are afraid to remove your mask! To step out and walk in the purpose God has already predestined for you.

The time is now to come from behind the mask to be vulnerable not for me, but for God. Today, I am inviting you to drop the mask and get real with me because like me, for years you have hidden behind the façade of perfection, acting as though you are all put together, so no one even you sometimes know your fears, your doubts or your innermost dark secrets. Trust me, I've been there. I have been just where you are, and if you are not careful, it will suffocate you. Like me, many of you reading this book look like you have it all together, trying to be Super Woman, Wonder Woman or even our girl, Sasha Fierce. Yet you are hiding behind masks of unforgiveness, depression, abuse, fear and failure; and up until now, you have been doing well holding onto your mask until "it" happens. The hand that is holding the mask gets tired and slowly falls away, revealing the true you for the whole world to see.

UNVEIL THE MASK

My flesh and my heart may fail, But God is the
strength of my heart and my portion forever.
~ *Psalms 73:26(NKJV)*

Pray and ask God to show you everything you have
told yourself about yourself that caused you to start
collecting your masks. Ask Him to reveal to you what
others have said about you that contradicts what you
know to be true. As He discloses these things to you,
search the Scripture for the truth, meditate on it and ask
Him to heal you where you hurt.

CHAPTER TWO

Moving from Blessed to Broken

EFORE WE CAN GO TO GOD TO FIX THE PROBLEM, WE will need to first understand what brokenness is.   The biblical term describes broken as a person who is extremely discouraged and unhappy, a person who often feels crushed and is living in a place of bitterness or someone who has a crushed spirit. I know, I know, that's not you because who would ever say out loud, "Hey look at me, I'm broken!" Or even want to be looked at as broken?   From the world's viewpoint, we see things that are broken as ugly, unwanted or of no real value; and depending on the condition it's in, we either try and repair it back to its original state or throw it away, right?

Like the Potter in Jeremiah 18, who finds himself remaking the pot because he was unhappy with the end result, God, the Creator of all things good when he sees us bruised, broken or marred; takes what you, I or the world sees as useless, ugly or broken and makes it over to the very thing we were originally created to be. That good and perfect being that he envisioned before we took our first breath. And more often than not, there is pain that comes with our makeover. You see, the way we see brokenness is the direct opposite of how our Daddy-God sees it. To him, brokenness is a process that brings about transparency. It's a process that allows our flaws to be exposed and brings us to a place where we not only, do not have the final say about the process, but when we really submit to being broken, we have absolutely nothing to say about the process except, "Yes, Lord, I surrender."

Looking back, I realize that my breaking process started in 2008. I know it now to be my Jonah period, a time where I was running from God and the call he'd placed on my life. And as I pen today's conversation, I didn't realize it until the day I received the first phone call from my client saying, thanks, but no thanks. While some of what I was experiencing had to do with subpar operational and financial management on my part, God was showing me, me. He was showing me that while I prayed for my business, I didn't include him in my business – and because he wasn't at the center of it all, it and my desire to be an entrepreneur had to be tested for authenticity, even to the point of being asked, "had I ever considered I was being considered?" I recall having dinner with my good friend Kevin, someone whom I respect a great deal for his business acumen. It was around the time my clients were calling to tell me how much we meant to their business, but despite their desire to continue working with us, a decline in sales would not allow them to continue the relationship with us. I was also working on a major business opportunity I knew was outside of my purpose, but had it prospered, it would have landed generational wealth for my family.

As Kevin and I talked, I told him my fears of potential failure and not knowing if I could bounce back from a hit like the one I would experience at the beginning of 2015, and he said something to me that I not only will never forget, but I remind myself daily to do. He said, "Sis, what our Daddy has for you, you already have it, but you gotta stop looking for it with your natural eyes and start seeing that thang with your spiritual eyes." Spiritual Eyes! Are you kidding me? What are you really saying? Smart he was, but probably too cool for his on good! Later that night after arriving home from dinner, I prayed just that. I asked God to allow me to see with my spiritual eyes what he had purposed me to do – to start seeing things the way he saw things.

How many of you know you have to be careful what you ask for, especially when you're talking to God? When we are sincere in what we ask of God, he delivers. And boy did he! A few weeks passed and during my prayer time, it was as though God Himself was standing next to me. As I began to think about all the hell I had been through the past few months, I began to cry out, "Lord, what is it that you want me to do!" Then I heard these words as clear as day, "What is your sacrifice?", "What is your sacrifice? What kind of the question is that to ask someone who's vulnerable? Who just lost over a half million dollars in revenue, I asked? Without giving it a second thought, I put my Big Girl pants on, and I blurted out "My business!" because I was afraid. Afraid of failing. Afraid of starting over. Afraid of what 'they' would say if I failed.

Your business? What did you just say? You can't give up your business? How do you give up the only thing you've known for the past decade?" That was my Chatty Kathy - - - the old me. The woman who said she relied on God to do it all for her, yet she made every move without consulting him fighting with the new me - - -

the woman who had committed just a few months earlier to walk totally and completely with God, trusting him for it all!

I was used to thinking I had heard from God, but this was a rare occasion that I knew without giving it a second thought that I had heard the voice of God as clearly as I had heard it that night. Now some of you know what caused your brokenness, so let me be the first to tell you that's the area of your life God will target and depending on the magnitude of our brokenness, like me, we fall into a state of depression. Do you recall the pain you felt as a kid when you fell and scared your knee? When that first real love broke up with you? Or when someone close to you went home to see the Lord? Like those, the pain you experience in times of brokenness is very similar. How deep the pain travels will depend on what is being broken and how long it has been a part of your life. Things like jealousy, pride, greed, lustful thoughts and actions they are all culprits of brokenness and while God doesn't cause brokenness, he will permit certain circumstances surrounding our brokenness to teach us and often times the lesson will be a public one.

Sistah, broken things and broken people are a direct result of sin. Every one of us has attitudes, habits, relationships and desires that are not pleasing to God. If any of those things are contrary to what God desires or causes us to sin habitually, that is an area that is susceptible to being broken. If we start to consider them more valuable than our relationship with him, it will be broken. Romans 2:15 tells us that God places in our conscience a nagging voice that tells us what we've done wrong and the Holy Spirit brings about conviction. Be it professional or personal, our relationships are one of the leading causes for being broken. When we try to substitute anything or anyone for him, he breaks it! Crushes, shatters and removes that very thing.

Our poor dispositions, bad attitude or whatever the case may be, all because of your inability to work through problems the right way, you ran them off and in an effort to repair "ourselves", we say, "They were only meant to be in our lives for a season" or "That wasn't the door God had opened for me!" Well, I stand here to firmly tell you that it is more of a lie than the truth! As much as we may think or have been taught to be an independent woman, our sole existence is dependent on him, God that is! He is the potter and we are the clay. Peter tried and He broke him!

Do you recall the story in the Bible of Peter walking on the water? There Jesus was walking and probably talking with God while on the water and Peter sees him from afar, calls after him and ask, "Master, if it is you, then call for me?" Well, in one single word, 'Come!' Peter's test began. On faith he steps out and begins to walk on water. He soon becomes engulfed with fear because he took his eyes off of the one who ordered his steps and begins to sink. Yep, you guessed it, Peter was broken to be taught to trust Him. Can you think of a time when you lost a job and you thought your wit, education or sphere of influence could land you a job, but turned out that they couldn't and what should have been a few weeks of unemployment was now almost two years? Now you are subjected to accept help from a family member, a friend or even someone who you weren't really close too? That was Jesus breaking you to remove pride. Or a time when someone you thought was a friend hurt you and you're asked to forgive, yet you question God and ask, "how many times do I have to forgive them?" and you recall in the Word where Jesus says to forgive 70 x 7? He was breaking you from self-righteousness. Well, just like Peter, there's an entire list of things that Jesus will do to break us bit by bit, situation by situation and trust me when I say the breaking process is not only deliberate, it's intentional. I heard my Pastor, Dr. Remus E. Wright, at The Fountain of Praise, in Houston, Texas, say in one of his sermons, "God will tolerate our weaknesses, but he will not tolerate our wickedness." And while I know all these things to be true, we just cannot seem to shake the pain that we have. Feeling the pain after a horrible loss or heartbreak can be devastating and we begin to ask, "Why me? How could God allow me to go through such pain if he loves me? How do you leave me here to deal with this on my own?" Well, the truth of the matter is that he doesn't. Deuteronomy 31:6 tell us to be strong and of good courage. To not be afraid or terrified because of them. Who is them? What's your them? I know sometimes it seems as though we are not worthy of God's grace, but you have to know that because Jesus died for you on Calvary's Cross, God is patient with you throughout the experience of brokenness. He knows all about you, where you have come from and how you got there. He also accepts and loves you unconditionally. Which means we don't have to work for it. He also knows how long it will take you to get it together and walk in the freedom that he's given to us through faith in His Son, Jesus. Well before your parents even thought of conceiving you, the Lord already knew who and what you would become and is committed to you experiencing all the blessings he has for you. While you, from time to time may experience some really tough times, and everything seems to be caving in around you, during the breaking process, God's intent is never to break your spirit. Remember, your breaking process is deliberate and intentional and is working out for your good. Over the course of the past twenty months, I've learned it's your will he's after and it's not until he can break your will that he can make you whole again.

UNVEIL THE MASK
The Lord is close to the brokenhearted; he rescues
those whose spirits are crushed.
~ *Psalms 34:18 (NKJV)*

Pray and ask God to show you your broken places. As
he discloses them to you, write them down and find
scriptures in the Bible that reinforce God's intent to heal
you in each of the areas he exposes as pain points. Post
them in a place where you will be able to see them
throughout this journey. They will be your spiritual
reminders and constant assurance that the Rescuer is
with you in the midst of the breaking process.

CHAPTER THREE

Dealing with Brokenness

THE FIRST STEP TO DEALING WITH BROKENNESS IS giving up control. I know you're independent and can do it all yourself. However, when we are broken God doesn't want us to take control. He wants us to relinquish total control to him and allow him to make us over. Here is a time when you can say, Jesus take the wheel and allow him to break you of self-reliance because of his love for you. Sure, you're afraid. What if He really doesn't know you like he says and gets it wrong? What if he has you doing something you're not comfortable with? Foolish you, I had the same thoughts. I felt the exact same way. Talk about crazy! Me and you that is! It's crazy to think the God who created us really doesn't know us. So prepare yourself and get ready for the ride, because when God sees there is a need for you to be broken, trust me, he will break you! And get this, it's his contract. He sets the terms and conditions on what needs to be broken and how it will be broken; and while it's going to seem like forever, just know the breaking period will not last forever. He's going to take you there, to a place where life will seem unbearable, and as bad as it may feel right now, he knows just how much pressure to apply. And get this, the beauty of it all is knowing he'll never allow you to get to a place where his ultimate purpose for your life is ruined. How long will it last you ask? As long as it takes for him to sense your true desire to obey his Word. It's that simple. The minute he can sense that what you say with your mouth matches what you feel in your heart is the minute he will ease the pain.

In yesterday's conversation, we talked about moving from broken to blessed, and as you recall we discussed how God targets the area that requires breaking - that he arranges the circumstances and decides on the tools to break us. We also learned it is he, who determines the length of time we go through the breaking process and more often than not, our brokenness happens because of the habitual sin in our lives. Well, he does this all in an effort to compel us to seek him and ask for forgiveness, so he can heal us where we hurt and make us whole again. Whether it's pain from jacked up finances, a job you lost, a relationship that abruptly ended, a death of a friend or loved one or personal failures, life can break us. And like Ruth, who called herself bitter, we fall into the trap of defining our lives by the hurt or imminent downfall we are experiencing, but the truth is God created us to have a better life. His promise specifically states that we will have life, and have it more abundantly. But we have to make an unyielding decision and conscience effort to not allow our past hurts to haunt us, and work toward living that abundant life! So how do you push past it, the hurt that is? The personal failures? Or that bad habit that haunts you? Especially when you feel as though you have called on him and he's not answering? How do you do this when it seems as though God has left you to deal with things on your own? You don't! God gives us assurance that you are not left to handle the problem on your own - that he is right there in the thick of it with you.

As I was preparing to write today's conversation, God led me to a very familiar passage in Luke 5: 17-20. In this passage of scripture Jesus forgives and heals a paralytic; and what I discovered is that before Jesus healed the man of his brokenness, he first had to forgive him. Like the paralytic, we too have to be forgiven before we can be healed. I'm not saying this man was paralyzed because he had sinned in some sort of way. However, what I am saying is, as with sin, disease is a form of evil that Jesus has the power and authority to expose for what it really is and declare God's opposition to its manifestation in your life. So before Jesus could heal this man, before he can heal you or me, he has to forgive us, because God's ultimate goal for this man and for you and I, is wholeness. One of the first steps in dealing with brokenness is to ask God to forgive you and make you whole again, then begin to focus on God's promises for your life. Promises that he will never leave you or forsake you, that all things, good and bad (that man walking out, the death of a close friend or relative, childhood molestation, lose of a job or whatever the case may be), work together for good to those who love him and are called according to his purpose. God promises that he is your refuge and your strength in the time of trouble and your provider. God promises that he will give you rest, he will guide you, and that he is the restorer of your soul.

I know, this seems like it's easier said than done, especially when you already know these things because you've been a believer for a while. You probably don't feel like you are worthy of his forgiveness. You may even think that I really don't understand your dilemma. So let me see if I can make it a little clearer, "Sistah, you gotta work that thing until it works!" Matthew 11:28 says, "Come to me all those who have labored and are heavy laden and I will give you rest." So, the question is, "Have you labored?" Have you gone to him like Hannah, in fervent prayer asking him to fix that thing? And are you trusting him to fix it or are you trying to solve the problem yourself? When we call on the name of Jesus, that's when God himself stands up and says, wait a minute, that's my baby calling! and it is then that he is mandated to stand up in our situation! When he does, heartache, disease, jacked up finances, personal failures and depression have to go! So stop trying to work out your problems without believing in and calling on the Problem Solver! Luke 5:18 says that the man was paralyzed, which means that he was totally helpless. He couldn't move. This man was completely dependent on someone else to take care of him. That's what brokenness does to you. It paralyzes and stunts your growth. You have no movement and you're left in a place where you feel as though you can't do anything alone. Oh, but thank God for this man's friends! He had a set of friends that were willing to ride and die with him! Friends who wouldn't let him wallow in his mess and the same goes for you and me! Like this man, you need friends who can speak a word of encouragement to you when you are at your lowest point - when you are bitter like Ruth, and your heart is empty, to help you get back to believing God like you used to! Friends who know and believe in the Power of God – and are strong in their faith. Friends who will be like Parliament Funkadelic and tear the roof off the sucka to get your promise from God! Friends, that despite how crazy it may be, will look at you and say, "Hold up, wait a minute, I'll doggone if I let you go out like that! Girlfriend, you may have lost your man, but you still know the Man! You may have had personal failures, but who is your Daddy? Talk about ride or die, the scripture said, "The men brought on a bed a man who was paralyzed whom they sought to bring him and lay him before Jesus." I can only imagine that these men traveled a long way carrying their paralyzed friend, because once they got there and realized that there was no place to put their friend, they looked at each other and said, "Bump this, we're not going back! We've come too far, he's gonna get to Jesus!!!"

Think about it, they carried this man. He couldn't have weighed no more than 150lbs during those times, but now in his paralysis, he feels like 300lbs of dead weight. So they were in excruciating pain from carrying their friend, and I'm certain they were exhausted from the long journey. But, these men and their crazy faith pressed, climbed and kept pushing until they got to the roof where they saw a way in and lowered their friend to a place where he was positioned right in front of Jesus! And the Bible says, because of their faith in believing he could be made whole again, God forgave the paralytic and healed him. So baby, you have to have some radical friends that will help you deal with what's broken in you because sometimes it's their faith, their prayer and their love for God that will get you through! Friends that will choose to fight for you when you can't fight for yourself, to motivate you and to say when you look like you can't make it, "I got you!" Like these five men, you have to choose to fight for what God promised you, and you have to be in the right place physically and mentally for God to bless you, because as long as you stay broken, you'll never reap the blessing!

As a kid and even in my adult years when I experience setbacks, I can hear my mom saying, "What are you crying for? Pull yourself up by your bootstraps and keep moving!" Sounds kind of tough, right? But what she was saying is get up and fight! So ladies, despite what this world throws at you, despite your thoughts being crowded with circumstances, get up and fight! Get your friends together and keep pushing until you have received that thing God has promised you.

Unveil The Mask
And the vessel that he made of clay was marred in
the hand of the potter; so he made it again into another
vessel, as it seemed good to the potter to make.
~Jeremiah 18:4 (NKJV)

Pray and ask God to show you everything you have told
yourself about yourself that caused you to start your
master cover up. Also, ask Him to reveal to you what
others have said about you that contradicts what He has
said about you and that you've embraced as truth. As
He discloses these things to you, write them down and
ask Him to forgive you and to heal you where you hurt.
Remember you are the righteousness of God in Christ
Jesus. Removing the mask and taking an honest look at
who you really are is the first step to fulfilling that call
to righteousness and being in right-standing with God.

DAY FOUR

Moving Past Fear

TODAY I INITIALLY WANTED TO TALK ABOUT the consequences of sin and how sin drives a wedge between God and us. But as God would have it, today I'll be talking about fear and faith and the constant battle between the two. The day I wrote this, I was traveling to New Orleans for a job interview with a national non-profit organization to become their next President. Now to many that sounds pretty good, but for me after meditating on this major move and all that I was going to give up (at least from my point of view), it invoked an unshakable fear of the unknown. Most of us know the cliché, Fear is False Evidence Appearing Real. If you're honest with yourself, you actually believe the False Evidence piece, but the truth of the matter is just like brokenness, we have to really understand what fear is before we can conquer it. I recently read that fear is a stronghold established in our minds trying to prevent you from doing a thing that is right for you or from being the person God has purposed you to be. That's why you have to take every thought into captivity and not allow the enemy to infiltrate your thought life.

God has not given you the spirit of fear, but of power and of love and of sound mind. A safe mind, a mind of good judgment with a disciplined thought pattern. When fear starts to set in you have to remind yourself that you have the power of God through the Holy Spirit to no longer be a victim of fear, and to no longer be afraid to step out and trust him. You have the power of God through Christ to make sound decisions based on what he has promised and confirmed in his word. God called each of you and gave you a purpose. "You were Created by Design" and it's not by our works but according to his purpose and his grace through Jesus Christ that you are able to do what you are able to. Because of this, you should be fully persuaded that he is able to keep what he has committed to do until the day of his return. You have to be so steadfast, immovable, unshakable and fearless in your faith that you believe the promises God made to you. To stop focusing on the promise, but the person behind the promise.

While fear may find a place in your life because of your natural temperament, it is not a part of your human disposition. This means it is not a part of your genetic makeup. You were not created to fear. You were taught to fear. Fear may have started in your childhood when you fell off a bike or when you were hurt by someone you love, but in either case, it was taught. It is a stronghold that is first initiated in the mind and it can if allowed, immobilize you. Behind every stronghold stands a lie - a place where God's Word has been subjugated to any unscriptural idea or personally confused belief, which means we have a way to control it; and if we want to subdue or take control of it and move forward, we have to learn how to overcome.

I can tell you that I really didn't want to talk about today's conversation, because this really invaded my think space. If it had not been for a conversation with a girlfriend and my conscience nagging me, I would have skipped right on past it, because I was afraid of being exposed. I was scared of showing you my weaknesses, my mistakes, and even my downfalls. Remember, I'm the girl who's accustomed to picking herself up by the bootstraps and pushing forward but like an onion, as you begin to pull back the layers you'll eventually find the heart of the matter. Here lately I wake up every morning practically afraid. Truth be told, even more so today than any other day. Afraid of what you may think after I've shared some of the innermost parts of me. Afraid of my car being repossessed, of my cell phone or Internet being turned off. Afraid, because at this very moment, I'm vulnerable. I'm left wide open for scrutiny, but today God has called me to be transparent and out of obedience, I am.

You see, at the time I journaled this conversation, I hadn't worked in 14 months, and the only money I had coming in was about $400 a month of which I paid my tithes, on my storage bill, gas for my car and shared with others when I could. And like I told you in my introduction, I was not an expert. I, like you would be growing through what I'm going through; using my personal experiences as a testimony so we can grow through together. When you looked at me, I appeared to have had it all together. Remember the mask? Well, what you don't know about me is that I've had 3- failed businesses, 1- failed marriage, 1- child I gave up for adoption and while it was the best thing that ever happened to her, I failed as her parent. I've failed at a plethora of relationships, professional and personal; and as I share today, I sit here in fear of "what if's." What if this time, things don't work out? What if what I say to you, I don't believe myself. All of which, if I am not careful, if I don't pick up my Bible to remind myself what God says, or to pray for strength at that very moment, I am filled with anxiety so much that I feel suffocated. My fears paralyze me. They make me feel like I can't, or I don't want to do what God has called me to do. So rather than doing what I am capable of doing, dusting myself off and starting over, I allow someone else to take it on. So I say all that to say, "I'm just like you!"

However, I am reminded of a sermon Pastor Wright taught on Grace from 2 Corinthians 12:9, where God said to Peter, "My grace is sufficient for you, for my strength is made perfect in weaknesses." And to make it personal, it says that La Tanya and the beautiful butterflies reading this missive, with all of our imperfections, we don't have to be perfect. When we start to think about our weaknesses, our failures and anything else that conjures up fear, remember we are made strong in him. Even if that very thing we're afraid of doesn't lighten up immediately, his grace alone is enough to get us over the hump. Now let's be real. It doesn't say that you won't stop having thoughts of failure pass through your mind or fear tugging at your heart. It does say that even when you do if you change your thoughts and start to believe what God believes about you and see things the way he sees things about you, even you, with your messed up afraid self will find safety in his arms.

I was on a call with a friend, and they'd shared with me that for one reason or another, they'd lost quite a bit, and they were afraid to start over for fear of getting it again and losing it again. My comment was, "I'm living that very same thing as we speak." You see, ladies, God has allowed me to start, own and operate quite a few businesses that on the surface appeared to have been great businesses and I'VE MESSED THEM UP!!! Something I did or didn't do caused them to fail and now that he's allowing me to "start-over" to reinvent myself,

I am scared as hell! But you nor I can get overwhelmed with fear. We have to keep pushing and being ever so careful to play the right stuff in our heads. We need to start seeing things the way God sees them and ignore the mess that we see with our natural eyes. The more you begin to believe, the more you begin to fill your mind with images of paying off those creditors, starting that new business, cleaning up your credit, forgiving that person that hurt you, or giving more; things will start to change! A shift in the atmosphere will start to happen, but it all starts in the mind! Romans 12:2 says, "and do not be conformed to this world, but be transformed by the renewing... [renovating...completely changing] of your mind for better." Someone said it takes a thought to heal a thought, so when negative thoughts start to creep up, remember Jeremiah 29:11, that God has thoughts of peace and not of evil, thoughts of hope and a bright future about you. Why shouldn't you also have them about you and your present situation?

As fear sets in recall Isaiah 54:17, that no weapon formed against you shall prosper, that you are more than a conqueror. When you are dealing with fear and overcoming it, you can't just throw something up against the wall and hope it sticks, you have to call on the Word of God. You have to be deliberate and intentional in applying God's word to your life. When you do, then you will begin to prosper wherever you go! So what you've messed up? Nobody cares but you and your haters. Who cares if that 1st, 2nd, 3rd and probably 4th business failed? Who cares if he dumped you or touched you when he wasn't supposed to? You have to keep pushing! Don't be afraid to start over, to reinvent yourself! Reinvention is good when God's included! It doesn't matter how many times you've fallen, it's how many times you've gotten up that make the difference.

It doesn't matter how terrible that last relationship was, remember God is there, and he will never leave you or forsake you. When you start to make Jesus the center of your life, God will cause his blessings, favor, and grace to begin to flow through and to you in every situation. The things you were once afraid of; will now become the things you've conquered. Then you can quote, "No Weapon" and mean it this time! Give your fears to him. When you begin to apply God's Word and call on him, he has no other choice than to stand up and come to your rescue, but you got to call on him.

UNVEIL THE MASK

"Be strong and of good courage, do not fear nor be afraid of them; for the Lord your God, He is the One who goes with you. He will not leave you nor forsake you."

~ Deuteronomy 31:6 (NKJV)

Fear is a crippling disease that often holds us captive to the lies of the enemy. It's time for you to put your "Big Girl" panties on and expose those lies that are keeping you from your destiny. Make a list of the things that you are afraid of. That's right in order to conquer a bully, you've got to face him. After you make the list, pull out your sword, (the Word of God) and find out what God has to say about the bully called FEAR. A good place to start would be Ephesians 6:10 – 17. Once your list is complete with your fears on one side and God's Word on the other, then you have your scriptural weaponry to fight the enemy any time those lies attempt to become your truth. Selah

DAY FIVE

I Am Designer Made

FOR YEARS I HAVE TRIED TO BE LIKE OTHERS, becoming a chameleon just to fit in. The price I paid was not really knowing who I was. Taking on the identity of others, was, in fact, camouflage. I was actually running from the one thing I hated most...ME! I hated that I was light-skinned. I hated that I had what my so-called friends called 'pretty eyes.' I hated my full lips and my nappy hair. All the things that I see today as beautiful, I hated and harbored resentment for them being my unfortunate lot in life. I wanted dark skin like my siblings so I could feel the love they felt for one another. Normal eyes, because my so-

called friends hated the one's I had; and nappy hair
because it was said that only ugly girls had nappy hair.

Now as an adult the fear of being accepted haunts me,
so often times I find myself overcompensating. But even
in my overcompensating, it never pushed me to fully
excel. I half completed everything. I wanted to show
people that if I failed at one thing, I was smart enough,
witty enough, savvy enough and let me not forget
resourceful enough to bounce back. My need to be
accepted caused me to make some terrible decisions, but
thank God for Jesus, right? For keeping me, for
protecting me, for sheltering me, for loving me even
when loving me wasn't my priority. Wanting to be
accepted caused me to give one child up for adoption
because of fear of what people would say about a young
mother, single with two kids, no real job, or education
and living off and on the system. Kind of petty huh? But
the reality is, I just wanted to be accepted, to fit in and
many of you who are reading today's devotional just
want to fit in too! Not knowing you are not supposed to.
Not knowing he didn't create you to be like anyone else.
Not knowing that before you were conceived he knew

who and what you would be for him, strategically created and uniquely designed for your God purpose.

Acceptance is something wanted by many, especially women. If we are not careful, we will look for it in all the wrong places. In abusive relationships with men you distinctly heard God say run from the day you prayed and asked Him, "are they what you want for me?" and he immediately says, "NO, RUN!" Yet you stay because he buys you nice things. With his mouth, he tells you he loves you, but with his hands he shows you how much he despises you. Wanting to feel loved, wanting to fit in, not knowing you were fearfully and wonderfully made. Knowing who and whose you are is key to living a purposed driven life. But because we are afraid to spend time at his feet, afraid to develop an intimate relationship with him and allow him to reveal to us his plans for our lives we find ourselves missing the mark.

UNVEIL THE MASK

And the vessel that he made of clay was marred in the hand of the potter; so he made it again into another vessel, as it seemed good to the potter to make

~Jeremiah 18:4 (NKJV)

The Potter's hands are skilled in rendering masterpieces; He won't stop until you reach perfection. You are God's masterpiece! Conformity is man's way of managing you. When we choose his way over our natural bend (the way that God designed us), our results are counterfeit. They never hold the ability to satisfy us, make us whole or even fix what's broken inside us, only the Master Potter can do that. Jeremiah 18:4 says that He can and He will. Do a check-up from the neck-up and identify what's counterfeit or an imitation in your life. For example, are you still holding on to the remnants of a past relationship, hoping that he will one day leave her for you and you two can be happy again? Or are you not fulfilling your obligation to your boss by withholding your best because you don't want to fail or because he gave the promotion you wanted to someone else?

Whatever it is, call it out and give it over to the Master Potter to make it into what He deems is good.

DAY SIX

The Blessings Behind Brokenness

FIRST SAMUEL BEGINS WITH THE STORY ABOUT this remarkable woman of grace, Hannah. Loved by her husband Elkanah, but due to her inability to have his children was subjected to a life of duplicity. She was living in a house alongside her husband and his other wife Peninnah and the children she was able to give him. The more I studied the text, the more I could relate to Hannah because despite being tormented by the other woman, despite the pain she had to endure of not being able to have her husband's children, Hannah's faith was unwavering. Her prayers stayed fervent. And I just have to believe that God placed her story in the Scripture as an example to show us that no matter what life throws at us when we exercise our faith and are fervent in our prayers that he will show himself to us even through our brokenness.

When I initially penned today's conversation, I immediately wanted to share with you how strong I was after experiencing multiple bruised relationships, both professional and personal. I wanted you to see that even with all that I'd gone through that I was still standing, but God said to me instead, while you want to tell them how you were bruised, but not broken, I want you to tell them about the blessings that come behind the brokenness... so today is about the blessings behind brokenness.

Blessed and broken, ha! How can this be so? Two words, when you look at them with your natural eye, they don't seem to go together. As a matter of fact, take a really good look at them. They are exact opposites and like Hannah, we all know what it means to be broken – to be shattered, to feel as though the bottom of our worlds opened up and there we were falling into a personal hell. A time where we couldn't eat. Couldn't sleep or even times when we thought the tears that were falling would never stop flowing. Broken. Shattered. Crushed. Filled with despair. These are all words we can use to describe Hannah's disposition. Broken, a void that cannot be filled. A sorrow that cannot be comforted, a wound that cannot be healed. But while your life may look somewhat broken today, that very thing that seems broken beyond repair will be the very thing that drives you to be more sensitive to his Word so you can hear him now in order to receive what it is he's promised you!

Now here is Hannah, who despite the love and adoration her husband felt for her was broken and filled with despair because of her inability to have his children. Can you imagine the hurt and pain she must have been dealing with day in and day out? Here the man of your dreams loved you, and you loved him, but the one thing that was standing in the way of total and complete happiness was your inability to have his babies! Not only couldn't she have his babies, but here she was living in the same house with her husband, the other woman and their kids. Broken! Hannah was living in an internal hell. You may be experiencing the worst time of your life right now, but it is at this moment that you must realize that before you can get to the blessings behind your brokenness, you have to know that the Lord hears you when you call. If you read the story of Hannah, you won't get past verse 10 before you realize she was in "bitterness of soul and prayed to the Lord and wept greatly," so while Hannah may have been the victim of Peninnah's torments, she didn't take on a victim's mentality!

She didn't walk around complaining, "Tell her to stop teasing me as Peninnah walked around rubbing her belly every time she was with child or when she would taunt Hannah with words that were meant to convince her that Elkanah preferred her because she was able to have his children!" Instead, the Bible tells us that Hannah said that's enough, I can't take it anymore, she got down on her knees and prayed in such a way that even the Priest thought she was drunk, when in fact what he saw was Hannah's desperation!

Her prayers were fervent, and her cry was "Oh Lord, "If you would just look on me this one time and remember me!" For every tear she cried, she pushed and prayed. But little did she know, that the more she cried and the more she prayed, God heard her and was starting to move on her behalf. He was preparing a blessing far greater that what she could have ever imagined! And that's what God is saying to you! He's saying yes, it's okay to cry, but push! It's okay to be hurt, but pray! Because as you pray and as you push I hear you, and I am preparing blessings that will far outweigh you're going through!

Not only does God hear you when you fervently call him, but you also have to know that even while the pain still hurts or that sometimes it may be too difficult to bear, that you are being processed to fulfill a bigger purpose! What Hannah didn't know is that through Peninnah's jealousy of Elkanah's unwavering love for her and her barrenness, God was processing her for purpose. Do you know that God will allow the very thing he hates the most to transpire to fulfill a bigger purpose in your life? So what does he do? He closed Hannah's womb and allows her husband and his other wife to bear multiple children – all to use her pain to bring about a bigger solution to a much needed problem that Israel was facing at the time.

Brokenness often times lead to insecurity, humiliation and will cause us to act out in ways that are ungodly, but we have to remember that even in our inadequacies or when people do things that hurt us, there is a right way to handle the problem. Had Hannah decided to fight with Peninnah, had she decided to whine and complain to Elkanah instead of looking to the Source, she would have missed it. Psalms 34:15 says "The eyes of the Lord are on the righteous and his ears are open to their cry." Had she gone about it another way, God would not have heard her. If we want God to remember us, we have to be like Hannah, fervent in our prayers. So while you may be going through a period where you're being processed for purpose; a period of brokenness, trust and believe that it is through your fervent prayers that God will hear, heal and give you multiple blessings behind your brokenness. Because the bigger purpose for your brokenness was for his glory and the building of the Kingdom.

Unveil The Mask

Cast thy burden upon the Lord, and he shall sustain
thee: he shall never suffer the righteous to be moved.

~ Psalms 55:22

Hannah's story is a beautiful reminder that God is
constantly listening to our prayers. Have you really
committed everything, even that thing that you perceive
to be impossible to be fixed to Him? If not do it today!
He sits on the edge of His throne and beckons you to
come. Won't you turn it over to the Rescuer, the Lover
of Your Soul today?

DAY SEVEN

Processed for Purpose

L ET'S TAKE A LOOK AT WHAT
FREEDICTIONARY.COM tells us about the word
processed. It says, "processed is a series of
actions, changes or functions bringing about a result."
As a part of my study for today's conversation, I was led
to Jeremiah 1:5, where it showed how much God cared
about me and how he put much thought into what he
would have me to be. Long before you and I were ever
conceived you were made to stand out! Remember
beloved that God "fearfully and wonderfully made" you
and with this same love, he processed you for His
purpose. When you look at the scripture, not only do
you see that God called Jeremiah to be a prophet, to
bring the kingdom of heaven on earth, but he was set

apart to be different to do something great. The same goes for you and me. Matthew 6:33, says "Seek first the kingdom and all things will be provided to you." That means, your job, your celebrity, your gifts are all platforms to fulfill that purpose. We only reap the benefit of our purpose when we are connected to the Source. Until you come to realize that you don't live life for yourself and understand you are being processed for purpose, God is going to keep working and working, sifting and shifting until you move into that place.

But what is it? What did he wire you for? What are you processed for? That thing that you can't stop thinking about? When you wake up, it's there? When you lay down, there it is again, invading your think space? Each one of you were created to serve a unique purpose in life. To do something bigger than you, something to give meaning or purpose to your life. You better believe me when I tell you that because you are this unique being, you weren't created to get lost in the midst of other people. He created you a purpose, with your own unique fingerprint. You were processed for purpose. Stop letting people tell you, you're average - that you are just like your mother or anyone else you know! While there may not be anything wrong with looking like these people, or you may have some of their tendencies, God created you to be different! Uniqueness my sistah, is a part of your genetic makeup. You are designer made, and the Designer made you a rare breed!

You can go into Nordstrom's and see 10 to 20 pieces of the same thing. Same color, same pattern, same style - that's because they were massed produced, however, if you don't want to see another sister in the piece you have on, rocking what you're rocking – you're going to have to go straight to the maker...the Designer. As you are reading this, if you don't get anything else out of this book, know this, you were not mass produced! You were created by the Designer and for the Designer to fulfill his purpose in your life! When you are being processed for purpose, you must have a definitive reason for your life. Accept what it is God is calling you to do because he is waiting in anticipation to see his Word manifested through you! He gets excited because he sees the greatness that you haven't seen yet! That you haven't walked in yet! When he is processing you, shifting you, changing you to bring about this great result, he shows you a vision of that thing that is to come! What is it that thing God has shown you?

As a part of being processed, when he showed you the vision and things got a little tough, problems started to occur and your so-called friends started to walk out, or you lost your job, like Paul in 2 Corinthians 12:9, you didn't like the pain you had to endure. When the pressure appeared as though it was a bit much or the path was questionable, you asked God to remove the thorn, to remove the pain. And if you didn't ask him to remove the thorn, plainly state, you got scared! Let me encourage you by telling you that yes, your pain is hurtful and yes, the road may be difficult, but the processing, the shifting, the changes you're going through are not just for you! What I've lost, my hurt or my pain, they weren't for me. They are for this moment right here, to be able to share with you what I've gone through and am growing through!

When God called Jeremiah, he in return says, "Lord, I know you're calling me, but I'm too young. Yes, it's me, but I don't have my degree yet. Lord, I know you're calling me to start this business, but I don't have any experience yet, and God says, who cares? (I'm paraphrasing a bit here) he goes on to say to Jeremiah, "Forget what you know. Forget how inexperienced you are, how inadequate you are and know that it is I, who knew what you would be capable of doing long before your mom ever knew what sex you'd be. And because I have processed you for purpose, I am going to make you shine! So suck it up and let God use you! Listen, God created you to be known for something. He said in Genesis 12:2, "I will make you into a great nation." I will bless you and make you famous, and you will be a blessing to others.

Rahab, the prostitute, was processed with a purpose! She risked her life to hide Joshua's spies and for my Bible readers out there, you know this prostitute ended up in the lineage of Jesus Christ! Mary, the mother of Jesus, was processed for purpose! Who knew this poor teenage girl, who barely knew how to take care of herself would be the one to carry and have the child who would rule the world? Moses, born, hidden in a basket as he journeyed down a river, covered in bushes, found, kept, housed and clothed by the daughter of the very person who wanted him dead at birth, he led the children of

Israel across the Red Sea into the Promise Land...processed for purpose. And you remember our sister Hannah? Married to the man of her dreams. She loved him, and he loved her, but because she was barren, was subjected to living with her husband, his other wife and their children, only to cry out fervently to God to give her a male child. She conceived Samuel, a prophet who would later anoint King David, processed for purpose.

I can go on and on with numerous counts of characters in the Bible who were processed for purpose, so don't think God can't take you along with your ugliness, all your inadequacies and make your name great! It is in your inadequacies that you find your purpose! Proverbs 18:16 says, "your gifts will make room for you." Do you know that God placed things in you that the world will make room for? So get out of your own way! So what he left, he looks good gone! Who cares if they talk about you, it's just free advertisement baby! When you are being processed for purpose, you have to be sensitive to God, daily because as he is processing you, as he is preparing you, he is going to show you that thing that is to come!

If you keep reading Jeremiah, He shows Jeremiah a rod of an almond tree and asks, "What do you see?" Now to the average person, it's just a rod, but to God because Jeremiah "saw it," he knew that Jeremiah was starting to recognize what was starting to take place. God was ready in anticipation, excited to see what was about to unfold in Jeremiah's life. Ladies, Jeremiah had started seeing things, not with his natural eyes, but his spiritual eyes. He started to accept the process of what was about to take place. The same goes for you. You have to recognize and submit to God's training. Submit to the process of being processed for purpose. Submit to change even to the point of total loss of things and people like our friend Job. Remember the hurt, the difficult times or the pain you're enduring is not for you, it is for a bigger purpose. What is that? When you are being processed for purposed, not only do you have to recognize and submit to God's shifting and changing you, you have to wait and listen for his instruction. People are going to try and come against you and try to stop you from doing what God called you to do. They will tell you what you are doing don't make sense, but during your period when God is processing you for purpose you have to be careful to wait and listen for his instruction. It is when you try and jump the gun to go ahead, before you are properly equipped, properly trained that you tend to mess up! During the process, you have to get prepared. Be diligent to seek him and trust the time when he says to speak that he will give you a word in season. Regardless of how inexperienced you are. How inadequate you may think you are God's grace is sufficient, because he has processed you for purpose!

UNVEIL THE MASK

Before I formed you in the womb, I knew you; Before you were born I sanctified you; I ordained you a prophet to the nations.

~ Jeremiah 1:5 (NKJV)

Do you know what God has ordained you to be for the glory of His kingdom? As you've studied the Bible, have you identified anyone whose life is strangely parallel to yours? In the pages of the Old and New Testament are testimonies of how God has processed His people for purpose. In today's assignment, I am asking you to "study to show yourself approved." Find that story and use it to remind yourself of God's good plan for your life. Selah!

DAY EIGHT

What is Your Sacrifice?

YOU KNOW, IT'S ALWAYS AN OVERWHELMING, yet humbling experience for me each and every time each day I prepare the day's conversation, because if you're paying attention, God has a way of showing you, you. Today I want to start the conversation with something I read on Facebook that led me to my topic from one of the Ruff Ryder's Lyrics, "It's on You, So Whatchu Gonna Do?"

Anyway, my friend who's a pastor in New Orleans stopped by one of his wife's favorite restaurants to pick up Sunday dinner after church. As he got out of his car there was a man standing outside of the restaurant who stops him and says to the Pastor that he only has two dollars and would he help him purchase food? My friend says, yes, they go inside and stand in line. When it was their turn to order, the Pastor says to the man needing help, "how much do you have?" The man replies, two dollars. The Pastor precedes to say, "okay, give me what you have and I'll add the rest." Instead of the man giving the Pastor what he had, he says, "NO, just give me the money."

In their ongoing conversation, the Pastor says, "you hungry right?" and the man said, "yes," but I thought you were going to help? The Pastor said, "that's what I'm doing" - - - and the man responds, "and you need my two dollars to help?" Pastor says, "of course, because I need you to use what you have; to do your part." And after going back and forth with the man, the man out of frustration, says, "never mind!" and walks out! In his frustration, whether his intentions were to eat or not, this man decided not to play a part in receiving the blessing he would have gotten had he simply participated in the process.

Ladies, like this man, many of us fail to reap the benefits, the blessings and the deliverance God is trying to bestow upon us because we too, do not want to participate in our own blessings. You desire the help, but you are not willing to commit any action in your own deliverance or breakthrough. You hear it all the time that this is your season of breakthrough, a year to recover, yet you fail to do what it takes to make your miracle come true. Just like the children of Israel in Deuteronomy 1:6, where the Lord tells them they've stared at their mountain long enough, to turn and take their journey, yet they allowed fear of a city built on mounds to block their blessing. You are allowing your fortified city, the thing you made bigger than it really is to block your blessing. You are your own worst enemy, so when are you going to get out of your own way and start participating in the process? So I'll ask you, "It's on you, so whatchu gonna do?" Is it that you're not ready for the next level? Are you not owning the blessing God said you can have? There are countless examples of people in the Bible that had they not made up in their mind, who had said to themselves, "it's' on me, what am I going to do? Who had not made up in their minds that they were going to the next level. Had they not did their part and participated in their own blessing, deliverance would have never occurred.

Take the woman with the issue of blood, she had exhausted any and all means of taking care of her issue. Had she not been determined enough and pressed her way through the crowd to touch the hem of Jesus' garment she would not have been made whole. The ten lepers, knowing they were doomed if they did and doomed if they didn't, participated in their own deliverance. They cried out, "Lord have mercy on us!" and the Lord said, go and show yourself to the priest and as they went...not when they go there, but as they went, were healed.

With some of us, participation starts simply as a mindset shift. Making a shift and saying "it's on me, so what am I gonna do?" It's a matter of right believing and knowing that God has already blessed you and you simply owning it. It's a matter of believing that IF "you" do, God will! What are you doing to participate in your own blessings? As a life and professional development coach, I tell my clients, "I can give you the play, but if you don't study the playbook, how are you going to win when it's time to get in the game." You have to be willing to be a part of the process and participate in your own deliverance. It's not anyone's responsibility to fill your cup, but yours. ET, The Hip Hop Preacher says it's best, "Winners win and losers lose," what are you doing to participate in the process to ensure you win? Who's in your top five playlist? And I'm not just talking about music here. What are you reading? 2016 is the year of Jubilee, which means it's a year to recover every good thing the enemy stole from you, but what good is knowing that if you are not going to participate in the process? It's time to activate your hustle and stop putting pressure on other people to do for you when you are not willing to make "A" step to do for yourself! Even the paralytic in Luke 5 participated in the process. Had he not been willing to believe that God would heal him and trusted in his friends who carried him for miles to get him to a place that landed him at the foot of Jesus, participating in the process, he wouldn't have been healed.

Here's your opportunity to have a "do over", but you have to be willing to participate in the process.

Ladies, it's on you, so whatchu gonna do?

UNVEIL THE MASK

But worship only the Lord, who brought you out of
Egypt with great strength and a powerful arm. Bow
down to him alone, and offer sacrifices only to him.

~2 Kings 17:36 (NLT)

What is your sacrifice? Pray and ask God to show you
what needs to go on the altar of sacrifice in your life?
There are some things that you have been holding on to
that should have been gone a long time ago. Well now
God is asking you to examine yourself and release those
things that have stubbornly held you back from
pursuing your destiny. These things may be good, bad,
or indifferent. If they hold the place in your heart that
belongs to God, then it's time to release them.

DAY NINE

Authentically You: The Woman Behind the Mask

ODAY, I AM INVITING YOU TO DROP THE MASK and let's get real. For years, you've hidden behind the facade of your acting as if you are all put together. So much so that no one even you can properly discern your fears, your doubts or your innermost secrets. Ladies, you've played role after role. Worn mask after mask, many of which were absolutely not meant for you. So when did it happen? When did it all begin? When did you become a Mask Aficionado? Was it when you lost your job? When he left you? When they touched you? When you gained a little weight and wasn't sure how the world would view you? Or were you on the brink of losing your business and you didn't want the world to know you were a failure? How do you remove your mask if you don't know the truth about your situation? How do you overcome the lie you keep telling yourself?

With truth, and that truth is the Word of God! The promises God makes to you. The Word of God tells us, that he shall know the truth, and the truth shall make you free. So the lie you keep telling yourself can be overcome if you know how to fight! And if it's the truth itself which makes us free then what is the truth? What are you telling yourself about you and the reason behind your wearing a mask? Just because something is said and even if you believe it doesn't make it any truer, right? So again, what's the truth about you? What are you believing about you and your situation? Money funny? The Word says in Deuteronomy 28:12, "...You shall lend to many nations, but you shall not borrow." Lost your job? It is written that it is God who gives you the power to get wealth. Insecure? I am fearfully and wonderfully made. Loss of a loved one? I am your Comforter; I will never leave you or forsake you. You get where I'm going with this? The Word, your words, have the power to remove your mask! Your words, the Word has the power to fight any demonic stronghold that has you thinking the way you do about you or your situation. So what they touched you inappropriately, your words, the Word has the power to forgive and live again! I know he left you. Your words, the Word reveals that it wasn't rejection, but God's protection! The Word of God is more than a nicely bound book you use as a centerpiece on your table. It's a living, breathing thing. It is Jesus Christ himself. The Bible says, "I am the Word, the Word was with God and the Word was God." Ladies, too many of our masks aren't new. The masks are, like the Word, a living, breathing part of our genetic makeup worn as our everyday costume or disguise from the hurts, the pain or any other fear of the world. We've worn them so long, we wear them without even realizing we have them on. We need them. We can't live without them. All of us do it. We put on a mask to hide parts of ourselves to distract what's really underneath. When we're tired, we slip on a mask of energy. When we're struggling inside, we put on a mask of happiness.

When will the mask fall off? The moment you agree to stand on your feet and begin to say no to the spirit of abuse, depression, the spirit of failure or whatever it is that has you hiding. I'm reminded of when I first went natural with my hair. In the beginning, I had to apply and often times reapply spray, oils, and gel to make sure it stayed moist. Just as with my hair in an attempt to make it work the way I wanted it, you have to make sure the thing you hide behind stays off. You have to put on the whole armor of God and keep it intact. When you do that, you have a shield of protection that can't be penetrated. Once you start to wear your shield of protection and call on the name of Jesus, you will soon find that you'll no longer need your mask, or it will suddenly fall off! Because Greater is He that is in you than he that in the world!

Here are two truths I've learned about wearing a mask. First, you can only hold your mask in place for so long before you are no longer invisible and people start to see right through you. Take the woman at the well. John 4 gives a great depiction of revealing this woman's true identity. You all know the story so I won't go into too many details. However, for the most part, because of her current living situation being married five times and now currently living with a man who's not her husband, she desperately tries to hide by filling her water vessels during the hottest time of the day instead when all the other women filled theirs. During those times, meeting at the well for women was a big thing. It was a time of fellowship. A time to see how things were going at home, to talk about the kids, the husband...you know about life. But she, this woman, tries to hide and fill up around noon. Yet, this time, when she arrived a man was there. Jesus was there, and he says to her (and if you read the text he doesn't ask her, it's more like a command) he says to her, "give me a drink!" Ladies, these four simple words started the process that removed her mask. As a Samaritan woman to a Jew, she was supposed to be invisible, but he spoke to her! Jesus broke the rule and broke the barrier and now, this woman who was supposed to be invisible, who was being talked about behind her back, who had heard the whispers and the murmuring about her being in a house with a man who was not her husband was no longer invisible. Because he "saw her and spoke to her." And that's what you need to realize that no matter how hard you try to hide behind that thing, you are not invisible! God not only sees you, but his love for you allows him to see through you! To take it off! Tell him what hurts!

Tell him how you're mad! Tell him you're scared! He knows! Stand up and refuse to be hidden anymore! And to do that ...

We have to be honest about what we're hiding behind the mask. Since He already knows what's hiding behind the mask, why don't you, like the woman at the well, acknowledge what your problem is and allow Him to provide for it? Let him begin to reveal the beauty of God's work in you. When you do that, the Word of God says, as you draw nigh to Him, He will draw nigh to you. He will start to show you all kinds of things about you. Who you are and what you are capable of doing.   Let Him make it better from the inside out, because once your inside is restored and made new then what's inside will begin to reflect on the outside. That's what is meant by God when He says, my Grace is sufficient for you. It's not just some passive scripture. Despite what you may have gone through or are going through, "You are fearfully and wonderfully made." Like the woman at the well, God knew she'd had five husbands. She was also living with one who was not hers, but he still loved her enough to invite her to experience his Living Water, and the same God that invited her to take off her mask and to be honest about her situation is the same God that says to you, "I want more for you. I want you to be more. To do more. To have more. To belong not just to yourself, but to Me," so ladies today, take off your mask. Stop hiding. Share your experiences with God and let him start to love you the way you're supposed to be loved.

UNVEIL THE MASK

Jesus answered and said to her, "If you knew the gift of God, and who it is who says to you, "Give Me a drink,' you would ask Him and He would have given you living water.

~ John 4:10 (NKJV)

The Samaritan woman recognized Jesus for who he was only after she attempted to have a conversation with Him. Now it's your turn to be authentically real with your Savior and receive God's Living Water. He holds the key to your re-birth as a woman of God. One drink from the fountain of Living Water and your life will never be the same again. I've asked you to remove the mask so that He can reveal the beautiful you that He created you to be. It is my desire that when He's done, you'll be able to look in the mirror and see who you really are. Take the plunge, receive God's living water and become all He's ordained you to be. Selah!

DAY TEN

His Timing Is Perfect

THROUGHOUT CONFIDENTIAL CONVERSATIONS™, we talk about removing the masks, the things that keep us from walking in our purpose. The other day, I found myself putting my mask of fear back on, and when that happens, I know that somewhere I'm not trusting God. The more I mature in Christ I become, the more I am able to recognize the issue when it rears its ugly head and ask God to reveal the area or areas where I hadn't given it all to him. Or should I say, where I am being impatient and not trusting his current provision for me? As God began to show me where I hadn't let go, he showed me how impatient I was to have everything yesterday, so today's conversation is dedicated to waiting on God's perfect timing. Despite how things look, despite where you are today, know that God's timing is perfect.

I know that's hard when you are growing through what you're going through. In those moments of difficulty, waiting is often accompanied with a restless longing for better circumstances. A better house, a better car, a better job, a better husband and anything else we desire, when God is saying in his silence, to be content! Trust that I know what I'm doing, that I know what I think and have planned for you. Believe me when I say I know who and what's best for you, so trust me. Trust that I will make your name great, and you will be a blessing. Trust, my daughter, in my provision for your life, while you're waiting for your recovery. Trust me, because I know you better than you know yourself and I know exactly what you need and will meet those needs in my perfect timing.

When you are solely dependent on God's provision, you have to be willing to rest and wait. Wait without murmuring and complaining, without coveting your sistahs blessings, without being jealous because he is doing a great work in your friend. Wait, without envy or selfish ambition; and rest so he can work. Wait and rest knowing that God will supply all of your needs according to his riches in glory. Listen, do you know when we are discontent, we are saying we have no faith in God's ability to provide for us? When the old you remember who you were and what you did, push past that and listen to the voice of God who is saying sit still and wait. I have something better for you that I am trying to give you! Daughter, you want a boyfriend, and I want to give you a husband. You want a new job when I want you to own your own company, but because you complain so much about what you don't have and are fighting against what I am trying to do, I am going to delay it because you refuse to turn from the things that are causing you pain. You have not learned to appreciate your current state. Instead of me giving it to you, I am going to give it to your children.

While you're waiting, learn to appreciate the manna until you're ready to receive the meat! Ladies, your perception is your reality. If you see where you are as an opportunity to do better, well guess what? That's what it is, however, if you see yourself in a place of despair, that's where you are. As a kid, my mom would always say, "A scary man can't win!" That holds true when you are believing God for something. You can't fight and win with fear, and you surely can't recover if you are afraid to take off your mask.

Unveil The Mask

My timing is perfect. For I know the plans I have for you, "says the Lord. "They are plans for good, not disaster, to give you a future and a hope.

~ Jeremiah 29:11 (NLT)

I encourage you to dream a little. Make a list of ten things that you perceive God wants to do in your life. After doing that, multiply your expectations by 100 fold! That's how much God loves you because you are His favorite daughter, we all are. Will you finally possess all that God has for you?

DAY ELEVEN

Tested for Authenticity

I N EXODUS 14, THE LORD INSTRUCTS MOSES, TO tell the children of Israel, to go to another place and rest between Migdol and the Red Sea. His instructions were very specific and were put in place to trip up the enemy to make the enemy feel as though the Lord had forsaken them; as though, he had left them alone without any help. There may come a time in your pursuit to recover when God instructs you to take an alternate route. To go to a place of unfamiliarity, that's not comfortable for you in order to get where he wants to save and deliver you. People may think you're doing too much, that you're all over the place, that you are confused, but be obedient and follow the path God has laid before you. Yes, it will look as though you're going the wrong way or like you've been there before, but follow the process. God is taking you the scenic route, so enjoy the view, he's only taking you that way to confuse your enemy.

Once you begin to follow the process, he will allow your enemy to pursue you. I know that sounds crazy, to do what he says, only to be haunted by the very thing you are seeking him freedom from, but trust him. Do as he say because it's a minor setback for a major come back! I know it is not the way you would have done things. I know you would have gone a different route and did things a little differently, but remember God is the Captain of the ship, the Director of your play. He is the one who will guide you out of the turbulent sea or write a different ending to your story. Follow the process, because it is a test of your faith to be obedient. Trust me, he knows what's going on. He knows the enemy will be hard pressed after you. He knows you are going to think sometimes you're caught between a rock and a hard pace, that the mountain in front of you seems too high to climb, or the thing you just left is in high pursuit to pull you back to what you thought you were delivered from. He knows you feel trapped and are suffocating, but the good thing when you're riding with the King is, you have options.

I'm reminded of the story of Joseph, the Dreamer and how God gave him dreams and visions of things to come. Specifically, the one about him ruling over his older brothers. However, before the dream could manifest, Joseph encountered difficulty. He was stripped of the robe his father gave him and was thrown into a hole to be deserted and eaten alive by wild animals. After a change of heart, his siblings did not want to have his blood on their hands, decided to sell Joseph into slavery and he was eventually imprisoned. Yet he never gave up on the dream God gave him! Despite what was going on or what he was going through, he kept his dreams in front of him. He allowed his dreams to fuel the fire to get closer to God, to ensure the dream God gave him would come to pass. Joseph prepared. He followed the process. A process many of us don't fully understand. A process that may have made him think God didn't quite know what he was doing, but he followed anyway.

Like Joseph, God has given each of you a glimpse of what life would be like for you if you trust Him, but somewhere along the journey, like Joseph, those you loved turned on you because of what God promised you! In some cases, they left you to die. Not necessarily physically, but emotionally and you found yourself in a hellhole dying alone.   Ultimately imprisoned in your mind and what you believe in. You are enslaved with bad thinking and have forgotten the dream God showed you! The excitement you once felt when He first showed you has left and because life happened you no longer keep the promise or the dream in front of you. But let me give you some encouragement, you may have gotten off track and drifted onto another road, but just follow the process. It may not look like God knows what he's doing, but keep going. You may even find yourself questioning the process, but trust Him and keep going.   You are closer than you think! It may seem as though you don't have any help in sight, just know on your pursuit to recovery, God may have an alternate route for you to save and deliver you.   Your enemy may think you're confused, but be obedient and follow the path God laid before you.

Yes, it looks like you're going the wrong way. It may look like you've been there before, but keep going. Once you begin to follow him, he's going to allow the pressure to lift up off of you...the enemy will no longer be able to pursue you! I know it wouldn't have been the road you would have taken, but how has that worked out for you before? Keep the dream in front of you and stay the course. Follow the process because you are being tested for authenticity. He knows what you are going through. He knows the enemy is hard pressed after you, but here's the deal. What I love about God is he never leaves you without options.

You can choose to surrender and go back to the hellhole you've been living in doing mediocre, being mediocre, not living because you are enslaved by the fear of success. You are enslaved by fear of moving forward or fear of leaving the old you behind to see who the new you can become. You can try and fight the battle on your own, ill-equipped to win alone and end up losing it all or you can stand and trust the one who has the victory even over your enemy; or you can stand still and see the salvation of the Lord, and let Him fight your battle.

Listen, despite what you are going through, remember what God showed you and trust in the fact that God will deliver you. You may be imprisoned right now but take pleasure in knowing that He will deliver you. That he will make a way for you, instantly, but you have to wait on him and be prepared for his suddenly! Be prepared for the miraculous! I know it's tough right not, but in the meantime while you wait on your suddenly, prepare yourself and be obedient, then move when he says move.

Are you prepared for victory? Are you prepared to win to recover? If you're not, get ready. Suit up. Gird yourself up, so that when the time comes for you to move, to win, to recover you've done your part and can rest while you allow him to do his part. Your faith in God is not a stagnant faith. It is a faith that requires movement. It requires you to do some work, to travail, to persevere, but in the end, you will be triumphant! You should have lost your mind. You should have been dead, but just like Job, you are going to get double for your trouble. God hid you in a secret place so that no weapon formed against you will prosper. Through it all, he gave you a peace that surpassed all understanding. You've come too far to turn back now. You have fought too hard to give up. Use your words, find your voice and know that your strength to endure is always equivalent to the very thing you are going through. God will not put more on you than you can bare, so trust the process and in the God, who orchestrates the process.

UNVEIL THE MASK

Don't be afraid, for I am with you. Don't be discouraged, for I am your God. I will strengthen you and help you. I will hold you up with my victorious right hand. ~Isaiah 41:10 (NLT)

Don't ever forget where true victory comes from, it comes from the Lord. Think about your past. You have fought many battles that you could not have won on your own? It's time to bring those things to your remembrance. Make a list of those impossible victories and pull them out when you are being processed. When you feel weak, discouraged, or defeated; remember the battle is not yours, it's the Lords', and He always wins.

DAY TWELVE

It's Working for My Good

IF YOU ARE A CHRISTIAN THEN YOU KNOW THIS scripture. You use it a lot, "And we know that all things work together for good to those who love God, to those who are called according to His purpose." But what does it really mean, 'all things' – according to his purpose.

I think this is one of the most overly used, yet misunderstood passages in the Bible. When you say all things work together for good to those who love God, we misinterpret the part that says those who are called according to his purpose. When we think of all things we oftentimes we think that God played a part in the bad that has happened to us. And as I meditated on the scripture, the Holy Spirit said to me yes, La Tanya all things do work together on one accord for your good, but God didn't cause all those things; good, bad and indifferent to happen. He can only take the credit for the good that happens in your life.

While God knew the bad and indifferent were happening, he doesn't cause them. He allowed them. Some of the things happen to us because of our sins, some because of our forefathers, Abraham, Isaac, and Jacob but all things were permissible. And even when they do happen he permits it so that he gets the glory when he turns it around and restore those called according to his purpose. So what happened may or may not be directly caused by God, but we have to rest in the fact that he knows it is happening. While it may be difficult or the situation may not change immediately, stay mindful of the fact that something good is going to happen. That's the working for your good part.

During this process desire him more, because whatever it is you're experiencing is working on one accord with the good that God has already predestined for your life. Despite the job loss, despite the sickness, the disease, we have to trust that God knows what he's doing in our lives – that he is doing a great thing.   Do you think God would allow you to go through what you go through without growth? Without good happening? Not only do we need to follow the process, but we have to trust the process.   We have to stop focusing on the promise and focus on the Promise Keeper.   The same goes with the problem.   Stop focusing on the problem and start focusing on the Problem Solver.

Then you have to love him.   Yes, there is a prerequisite to receiving the good in spite of what's happening in the "now" of your life, you have to love God.   I'm not saying that if you're a sinner or if you're not saved that good won't happen because God is a merciful God.   I'm not even saying you have to work for it.   What I am saying however, is there are consequences for the things we do.   But, mercy and grace are the two things working in tandem for your good so you can come to know who he is in order to save and restore you again for his glory.   His desire is for us to do right, to love acting righteously and to walk with him.

Unveil The Mask

And we know that God causes everything to work together for the good of those who love God and are called according to his purpose for them

~ Romans 8:28 (NLT)

Okay, now that we know that God uses everything we experience for our "good," let's take a magnifying glass to your life and identify events, situations, and circumstances where God has blessed you beyond measure. I know He has, and you do to, so make a list. Break it into three categories: What He Has Done; What He Will Do Based on His Character, and What He Has Promised to Do! Have fun, you've been working hard, you deserve it.

DAY THIRTEEN

Single, Successful & Satisfied

IT'S REALLY FUNNY HOW THINGS HAPPEN IN YOUR life. Once you start to pay attention to what's happening, the subtleties, the bread crumbs here and there, you'll soon realize that everything was a deliberate and intentional act of God.

I know some of you are probably thinking, "How in the world can I live single, successful and satisfied when everyone is either married, in happy relationships or boo'd up?" Well, I'm here to tell you that you can! While the world or the married person you know may view your singlehood as a place filled with loneliness or incompleteness, the very place you're in today, this very moment of your singleness is the place where you're supposed to be. But it is not until you learn to define your state of singleness with God instead of without God that you will truly begin to accept being single and all it has for you.

Ladies, I need you to understand that the very state you're in today is tied to your calling; the divine condition in which one finds themselves. When you start to walk according to the purpose God has called you and begin to look at your state as a calling divinely ordained by God, then you won't be so quick to try and change it. Each one of you were processed for purpose. Created to serve a unique purpose in life. To do something bigger than you could ever imagine even while single! You were not massed produced. In fact, you were created with your own unique fingerprint - designer made by the Designer himself. So many people miss out on the joys of being single and all of its goodness because they are too worried about getting married.

What is your purpose? What is that thing that is keeping you up at night? What's stopping you from getting there? What are the things you can do now that when you get married, you won't be able to do as much or not at all? That's the thing you're supposed to be doing single! I'm not saying you're not supposed to date, but during your state of singlehood keep the main thing the main thing. Be single and successful while you're waiting on him to show you your Boaz and love it! But how do you do that when others view life without being married as a life with no meaning? How do you do that when you don't know your worth? How much you cost? That you were bought with a price? That you are worth far more than precious rubies? How do you live single, successful and satisfied?

One way is to wait. Don't be discouraged and by all means be content. Where you are right now is God's place for you. Dr. Tony Evans said in one of his sermons that God doesn't want singles out there mate-hunting. And quite frankly, it's true. Think about the guys you've found yourself with, I'm laughing because I just told a friend that as I look back at all the crushes I had over the years, I thank God, because he knew me! He knew those jokas were nowhere near my caliber of dude, but because I was doing the hunting my vision was slanted. So ladies, enjoy the season. It's a time where you get to know you. A time where you get to fall in love with God and when you get to that place where you're so in love with him that you've forgotten you're not dating, then it'll happen. You'll find yourself on a path that your Prince just happen to be on and like that, it's a perfect match.

But here's how we mess up. We compromise the plan and as long as we are compromising the plan, God will not help. We try and change our state for God when he doesn't need our help. We hook up or should I say, "shack up" allowing him sample the milk without any hope of him buying the cow. We allow him to put us on lay-a-way, only to put a down payment of what him think he wants only to realize there was a better deal around the corner. Someone who knew her worth and decided she was worth far more than rubies. Someone who said no to being second best when she knew she was designer made. Ladies, if you're living a compromised life, you know the one like I just described, you're compromising the plan so stop asking God for help. Stop asking for a husband when you're pretending to be wifey.

It was not until Adam was totally occupied with the things of God and God saw that he was content in the state he was in, that he gave Adam a helper. Before you rush to get married or in some instances as my mom would call it "shack" with someone analyze situation and ask yourself, "why do I want it so bad?" Then make yourself more valuable. This is a time where you should devote more time to sharpening your skills and developing your gifts and talents.

God knows the desires of your heart because he put them there if we're in constant communion with him. He knows how you're feeling and what it's like to be lonely at times. Increase your worth! Don't reduce your worth jumping in and out of relationships that God didn't ordain, because every day you spend with someone God didn't ordain is a day you don't get to spend with the one he did. So be patient and allow your Kairos (season) and your Chronos (time) to merge, because until they do you and you have work to do.

Unveil The Mask

Brethren, let each one remain with God in the state in
which he was called.

~ I Corinthians 7:24 (NKJV)

Stay the course. Being single, successful, and satisfied is
not easy in today's world. But with God's help, you can
do anything! Put your strategy for living a successful
single life on paper. Pray and ask God for his guidance
and watch Him work.

DAY FOURTEEN

Keep Pushing

T HE ENEMY HAS A WAY OF REALLY GETTING into our heads when he knows our breakthrough is just on the other side of the door. He throws thoughts of defeat, thoughts of fear and the "I" cant's into your head. He has a way of planting the seed where you are the one who's thinking that it's your thought, and you conjured it up on your own. However, God has opened the doors and windows of heaven to your blessings, your breakthrough, deliverance and your healing, but some of you will not receive it because you are afraid to walk through the door. Like me, you are afraid of what your future holds. You are afraid of starting over. You are afraid of standing out and being different. - of who the new you will become, but as you go through this day, I want you to stand firm, put your big girl pants on and tell yourself to 'keep pushing!'

Push your way to your breakthrough. Yes, it hurts, but keep pushing! You're tired, but keep pushing! I know it doesn't feel right, but you can do all things through Christ Jesus who strengthens you, so keep pushing! What are you afraid of, that's keeping you receiving all that God has for you? The new you is on the other side of the door, and she looks good on you! What are you allowing Satan to plant in your life and you're fertilizing, allowing it to grow, that's keeping you from your breakthrough? What cliques or wrong thinking are you clinging too that's holding you back?

In order to get what God has for you, you have to be deliberate and intentional with what you are feeding yourself or allowing to be fed to you. Stop getting full on defeat! Stop getting full on the lies they tell you and push! You've been pregnant with purpose, some of you for decades. And for those of you who know anything about childbirth, it's a difficult task, to say the least. Sometimes the baby comes without instruction, but sometimes you have to help them out with a little push because even before they have entered the world, they are stubborn. They are lazy. They are afraid of what they don't know, so you have to push!

Sistah, you have too much riding on this thing to stay where you are! In order to be outstanding, you are going to have to STAND OUT! You can't be the same person you were before. Stop fighting to be who you were and come to grips with who you are. Remember, you can do all things, but you have to activate your faith and push! When you know the truth, it is the truth that will make you free. The day you saw what God saw, the truth about you, you became free to do it! Be it nine months ago or just yesterday, the day you saw what God saw, he said he was not going to let you not get it, so he's pushing you. He's shifting you. He's sifting you.

The door's open, walk in it. The womb is open, give birth. Yes, you are feeling some pain. I know you're afraid of how the baby will look. Will it have all its fingers and toes? But just like in the birthing process when a baby who is trying to enter the world, there is a struggle. Your pushing is going to cause you some tension, some stress, even anxiety, but when you see the truth, you will feel grateful for the process that you had to go through to receive such a glorious gift.

UNVEIL THE MASK AND PUSH

The earnest prayer of a righteous person has great power and produces wonderful results.

~James 5:16B (NLT)

Have you ever been in that place where all you can say is "Jesus?" Well, I have, and believe it or not that was enough to launch 1000 angels on your behalf. Prayer changes things! It changes us; it changes situations; it changes the hearts of others, etc. This list can go on and on, but the point I want to leave you with is that sometimes ... No, every time you should pray until something happens. Speaking of lists, why not take a few minutes and write down your most urgent prayer requests. When God answers them, put the time and the date He does it so that you can go back when you are in the birthing process and remember His faithfulness in taking you to the other side of your deliverance. So remember the PUSH Principle: Pray Until Something Happens.

DAY FIFTEEN

In The Meantime, While I Wait

WITHOUT QUESTION, ONE OF THE HARDEST things for Christians to do with the Lord is to wait on his timing to make certain things happen in their lives. It is when you try to move ahead of God's timing that you find quickly that everything will fall apart and completely unravel. Even now, you may have some questions. Earlier I discussed how you should consider your singleness at this Kairos moment divinely ordained by God and by now you may be asking God, "What do I do in the meantime?" In my waiting period how can I be placed where I can be seen? Where he can find me?"

One of the first things you should know is that while you're waiting don't rush the process. Don't let the devil trick you into feeling like just because your friends and everyone around you is getting married that you should too. Wait on God. I know I come across like being single is easy breezy. When in fact being single, coupled with being a Christian and trying to live, breathe and walk like Christ is hard as heck! Like you, I have to be prayerful about my walk. I Corinthians 7:37 says "But if he has decided firmly not to marry and there is no urgency, and he can control his passion, he does well not to marry." What that means is we must consciously turn away from using other resources that we can turn to. I Peter 5:6-7, says, "Therefore humble yourselves under the mighty hand of God, that He may exalt you in due time, casting all your care ..." (Care denotes distractions, anxieties, burdens, worries - - -all are unnecessary because He already knows what we need) upon Him, for He cares for you. So while you're waiting, in the meantime, you should prepare both spiritually and physically for marriage knowing that none of the preparation time is ever wasted time.

During your meantime, solidify your relationship with God, draw close to Him and He will draw close to you. A dear friend of mine says quite frequently, "Any good relationship that will last has to have a strong foundation spiritually. While the person they are expecting God to bring their way doesn't have to have a walk as strong as theirs, they do have to be walking along the same path." So while you're waiting, spend time in his presence and get to know him intimately. While you're spending time with the Lord, he will renew your strength. Then learn how to pray. Many of us, me included are praying for the wrong things and praying with the wrong motives. But once our hearts are right, we should pray fervently.

Begin your process in prayer with the first step being to commit yourself to God's will. Which means finding pleasure in knowing and trusting him to give you the desires of your heart; the mate he knows will delight us further. While you're waiting, learn what you want in a mate. What's on your list? Once you learn how to pray, engulf your prayers with what you want and be specific! Tell God exactly what you want, but be clear on the biblical character of a godly mate. You should seek someone on a spiritual level and not just because they are attractive. If God told you that today is the day, I'm going to give me your mate. What do you want them to be like?

Another important posture to assume when waiting is to study and feed your spirit. It is important as Christians that we feed our spirit with the Word of God, so the time you're spending in the Word you are allowing God to speak to you and build you up spiritually. It is his desire to direct and guide you in every aspect of your life. Know the Word of God. Study it! Memorize it! The Word of God is a living breathing book that speaks to us in every area of our lives.

What are you feeding your spirit-man? I can honestly tell you that my life changed when I started to add teaching CDs and spiritual music to my daily regimen. When I'm having a moment, when I am feeling weak, Dr. Tony Evans goes directly in my ear and Juanita Bynum fills the room with her melodic sounds.

Find what works for you, but consider the spiritual food you're feeding yourself. If you're always listening to "stuff" that has you feeling a certain type of way, change the channel. If you're constantly watching things that get you in that space, turn it off. You have to be disciplined in preparing yourself spiritually. The things of the world and of Christ can't dwell in the same house.

Faith cometh by hearing, and hearing by the word of God. In order to have faith, you have to trust him. If we don't trust God, we will eventually become bitter human beings. We will either believe that he will give us the desires of our hearts or not. So when you start to lose sight, think about and remember God. While you're waiting spiritually, you must also prepare physically. If you desire to be married, and you are believing God to send you a mate – realize the importance of preparing yourself so when Mr. Right shows up you're ready. Are you an adequate match for the person you're believing God for? What are you doing to prepare financially? While you're in your meantime, are you being a good steward over and practicing good stewardship of what God has given you?

God gave Adam a job first, then he gave him a wife. But I also think that it wasn't until Adam learned to be a good steward over what he currently had, which was the garden, that God could give him something else. Adam couldn't have Eve as his wife because he was going to have to learn how to take care of her as a good steward!

Ladies, discover and develop the things that you like to do professionally and personally. Start enjoying your freedom now - learn how to cook. Moses spent 40 years tending sheep before God called him to full-time ministry. Abraham had waited for twenty-five years before Sarah gave him a child. And while I'm not saying it's going to take that long, what if it does? What are you doing to renew your faith in God in the meantime? I read the other day that waiting is not incidental to faith – waiting is the DNA of faith.

Even when it seems like He's forgotten, He is still in control. Habakkuk 1:5 says, "Look among the nations and watch – be utterly astounded! For I will work a work in your days which you would not believe, though it were told to you." So to us, it may seem like while we're waiting nothing is happening. It may seem like God has forgotten your prayers, but just know that he's behind the scenes working out something so good that it's going to blow your mind.

Redeem your time in the waiting room of life. Just because you're waiting don't mean there's nothing to do. Read books on relationships. Develop yourself – start praying for your future spouse (remember this is the only time you can worry about a spouse is when you are praying). While you're in the waiting room, that's your time of development.

UNVEIL THE MASK

Therefore, humble yourselves under the mighty hand of God, that He may exalt you in due time, casting all your care. (Care denotes distractions, anxieties, burdens, worries - - -all unnecessary, because He already knows what we need) upon Him, for He cares for you.

~ I Peter 5:6 (NKJV)

Allowing God to do a perfect work in you while you are a lady in waiting is one of the best moves you will ever make in life. Number one, it will stop a lot of drama in your life and the repetition of failed relationships. A heart-broken over and over again can only become a badly broken heart. The beauty of having a relationship with God is that no matter where you may find yourself, busted and disgusted, heartbroken and left to languish in your tears, He's there! The minute you say, "Okay God, I messed up, and I want a new start," He's there! Even if your heart is about to beat its last beat because it's so bruised and beaten up, He's there to give you a brand new one! Not only will He give you a new one, but He'll put you back on track for your promotion. So if you are in a place where you need to humble yourself, DO IT NOW!

DAY SIXTEEN

I Surrender All

ROCESSED FOR PURPOSE. BUT WHAT DOES BEing "processed" really mean? A series of actions, changes or functions bringing about a result. In an earlier chapter, I shared that even before you were ever born, before you were ever considered being conceived by your parents - you were Created by Design. God knew you, sanctified or set you apart, then ordained or chose you by divine appointment to be a prophet to the nations - - - created to serve a unique purpose in life. A purpose far greater than you and I could ever imagine. When He did this, he gave you your own unique fingerprint. Which says you are nothing like anyone else. That you weren't mass produced. You Are Designer Made.

When you are processed for purpose, you have a clear reason for your life and it is your responsibility to accept what it is God is calling you to do. When He is processing you, shifting you, changing you to bring about this great result through you. Like Jeremiah, he shows you a vision of that thing that is to come! But then like Paul, you don't like the pain, you can't stand the pressure or the route God decides to take you on and you ask to remove the thorn. Surrender and submit to the process of being processed for purpose. You have to recognize and submit to God's training. Submit to change. Even when what He's showed you in a vision and it is not clear to you or when it seems mystical to you, JUST DO IT!

But in order to submit you have to first surrender and not just some stuff, but it ALL!!! Which leads me into our devotion for today. Processed for Purpose: I Surrender All! And if you are like me, when I think of surrender I think of some of the old westerns my mom use to watch and the good guy is chasing the bad guy until the bad guy finally gets to a place where he is closed in...has no place to run...and the good guy, usually the sheriff tells him to give up! To surrender! There's no way out but through me! And then finally the bad guy surrenders. Like the Sheriff, God is saying surrender, there's no other way out, but through me!

It was around September 2015 when one of the ministries at The Fountain of Praise here in Houston was hosting a prayer clinic. While I didn't know what would happen at this prayer clinic because I'd never gone, I knew I would be blessed. I took my pad, pencil and coffee and left ready to take notes - - - it was great! Impactful prayer, great speaker and true deliverance was in the room. But while I was there, the heaviness I'd been feeling for weeks, if not months had come over me again so I went for a second time to have another minister pray with me. From what I gathered, a few minutes had gone by and I was now sitting with one minister behind me in the Lamaze position and she's whispering you're not letting go...you're still holding on...and then I hear this voice in my ear. I recognized it, but I can't seem to put it together because I am clearly in the Spirit and I hear the voice say to me, "I hear the Holy Spirit saying, "TOTAL SURRENDER! TOTAL

BLESSINGS!" I immediately knew what the Holy Spirit was telling me through this person, but I didn't want to give it up. I couldn't give it up. How do I give up what I'd known for so long? It was who I was, so I rebelled. I'll surrender this, but not that Lord! I'll give you this, but not that Lord! And this tug-a-war with myself went on for a few minutes until God said, "I've had enough!" I totally surrendered and once I did, I gave a loud cry that felt like I'd given birth only later to be told that my cry was the sound of a baby being born.

So, as you're reading today's conversation, Surrender! Whatever that thing you've been holding on to. That thing that you've been doing for so long; that thing that made you, you! The thing you've been trying to give birth to or been running from, surrender. Surrender it all and allow God to complete what he started in you! When God is telling you to surrender all because I've processed you for purpose don't be afraid of what he's telling you you're about to give birth to! In Luke 1:13, the angel came to Zacharias and said him, "Do not be afraid" for your prayer is heard, your wife Elizabeth will bear (become fruitful...will have activity) a son and you will call his name John (whose name means The Lord has shown favor)."

Then there was the Virgin Mary, the angel came and said to her, "Do not be afraid for you have found favor with God." Can you imagine being a young teenage girl who had already been promised to marry not ever being with a young man and being told you are going to give birth to a child...and not just any child, but the Messiah? Before you were ever conceived, God already impregnated you with what you're about to give birth to. It's time to give birth!

In your spare time, I want to encourage you to read Genesis 29 and 30 that tells the story of Jacob and Rachel.   The Word of God says, "Then God remembered Rachel and God listened to her and opened her womb." You might be reading today's devotion and may have been barren for some time now. You have not been able to give birth to that thing that God impregnated you with be it a few months, a year or even decades. You've lost your swag, but God is about to open your womb! It's time to give birth! It's time for you to start producing again, to be active again to get to a place where you're fruitful again, but you must first surrender it all! What's that thing you've been laboring over? You've cried out day in and day out fervently in prayer and God has not answered? Well, like Rachel, he has remembered. He listened, and your womb is about to be opened!

Like Mary, in Luke 1:38, embrace the process and adopt an attitude of complete undeniable surrender to the Lord. While I don't know what you're doing. While I don't know what you're fully up to or Lord, while this thing you've impregnated with me seems crazy to me, I trust you! I submit to you! Just like in the westerns, you have to throw your hands up and shout I Surrender! Because I know the thoughts you think toward me, thoughts of peace and not evil, to give me hope for a future. It's going to take immediate obedience on your part! Whatever he says to you, DO IT! It is only when we're obedient that God will open our wombs and loose what we've been carrying for so long. The womb is open. It's time to give birth, but you have to first SURRENDER IT ALL!

Unveil The Mask

Surrender your heart to God, turn to him in prayer, and give up your sins even those you do in secret. Then you won't be ashamed; you will be confident and fearless.

~Job 11:13 – 15

Surrendering your all to God is only a prerequisite if you belong to Him and have confessed His Son as your Lord. As Lord of your life, He has a right to expect your total commitment. Read Mark 10:17-27 to find out Jesus's expectation and response to the rich young ruler who wanted to serve Him, but ... Are you also holding on to some "buts?"

DAY SEVENTEEN

Change My Identity

FROM THE DAY I STOPPED RUNNING AND ACcepted the call on my life, I've never hesitated to ask God to show me, me. Knowing that when he did, there would be things I'm almost certain, I wouldn't like. As fate would have it one Saturday morning, I asked, and He delivered, but in a way that had me in a fetal position crying. And there it was as bright as light, he shows me, me in the word "acceptance," and every incident in my past where I fought to fit in. Not the girl whose mantra was to never let 'em see you sweat! But how can this be? I'm strong! I walk tall and talk like I can back it up! Here I was,

Sasha Fierce herself, having a need to be loved, to be accepted.

Not only had I been running from my call into ministry, but I was running from me! For years, I tried to be liked by others not knowing who I really was. Trying to fit in, taking on the identity of others. Being a chameleon, as I so lovingly called myself when in fact I was running from the one thing I hated most...me! I hated the color of my skin, I hated that I had what my so-called friends saw as 'pretty eyes,' and I hated my full lips and my nappy hair. These are all things that my Creator gave me to make me the beauty that I am, and I hated them. When I looked up the word acceptance, it was like a punch in the gut. It clearly said, the action or process of being received as adequate or suitable, typically admitted into a group. The more I studied the definition, the more I began to sink. That was until I heard the voice that said, "Be who I created you to be! You weren't created to fit in."

Ladies, the gifts God gave you are your gifts, and they will make room for you when you begin to use and perfect them. Know this, that if not one man accepts you, you are accepted in Christ Jesus. You were already approved by him and are graced with grace in him to be whatever it is he told you, you would become. Stop trying to be what and who you are not! Do you know that you are doing yourself and the God that created you a huge disservice by being anything other than what He created you to be? I said in a previous chapter that to many of us, masks aren't new; that they are a part of our genetic makeup worn as our everyday costume or disguise from hurts, pains or fears. We have worn them so long, we need them, and if you really give thought to it, you have one for every illusion you want to create. And if you are like me, you change them at the speed of lightening. So much so, we forget who is really behind the mask. We put on airs trying to be like someone else and for the most part, we have done well. We've mastered the art of 'masking,' but Jesus calls us to be more, to do more and to have more. He's called us to belong and not just to ourselves, but to Him.

When you look up the word renew, the word suggests a renovation, restoration, and transformation. A change of heart and life. A change for the better, an adjustment of one's moral and spiritual vision. When you renew your mind, you are allowing God's redemptive power to take that which was old (a wrong thought about yourself, a wrong belief, an incorrect way that you've viewed yourself) and restore it back to the original state in which he created it.

However, you can't renew yourself without renewing how you think. You will have to take control of your thoughts, as well as your wrong mindset or feelings about a thing. So when you are being renewed by the transforming of your mind, it's real meaning is you are literally changing how you think or feel about something; your thoughts, your actions, your purpose in life and your character. It's going to require you to abide in a right relationship with Christ and submitting totally to the unction and urge of the Holy Spirit. Paul says in Romans 7:21, "...desire alone to do good is not enough to fight the flesh, we have to war against the flesh."

The old you will fight the new you. The old you won't want the new you to shine, that's when you will have to use your words – the Word of God to ward off the old thinking. Your old lifestyle will tell you that your new lifestyle won't fit. Well, you weren't created to fit! It is not enough to just take off the mask of unforgiveness, depression, fear or failure, you have to be diligent to replace what you take off with good thoughts for success. Thoughts of happiness, forgiveness, that's what meant by renewing your mind. To redirect your thinking govern your thoughts to say good things about you.

When you take off the old things – the mask, you will still see yourself as the old you. It's not until you begin to renew your mind, in your spirit that what was hidden behind the mask will change and become a new creation. The longer you wear your mask, the more out of touch you are with the reality of who you are. You can't think straight anymore, causing you to be double-minded. The pain you feel is numbing, and you eventually lose all care. Everything connected to the mask, the old way, the old you have to go! Then start to work yourself in a way that accurately produces God's character in you. No more lies to yourself about yourself. No more faking the funk. Tell the truth about who and where you are and watch God meet you right there.

Be persistent in your pursuit of Godliness and commit to godliness with relentless persistence. Think about what you are thinking about.

Unveil The Mask

Don't copy the behavior and customs of this world, but let God transform you into a new person by changing the way you think. Then you will learn to know God's will for you, which is good and pleasing and perfect.

~Romans 12:2 (NLT)

Develop a strategic plan for renewing your mind. Identify the areas that you need to change, we all have them. Search God's Word for His perspective on that particular weakness and memorize that scripture and add it to your arsenal to change your thinking and renew your mind. Like medicine prescribed by a medical doctor, focus on these scriptures three times a day until they become your natural response when dealing with those problem areas in your life.

DAY EIGHTEEN

The Promise is Still in Affect

WHAT HAS GOD PROMISED YOU THAT YOU haven't received? Was it a house? A car? Financial healing? Enlarging your territory? What was it? If you haven't received it, I'm here to tell you that the promise is still in effect! You have dwelt at your mountain long enough, it is time to turn around and take the first step of your journey. Like the children of Israel, I had a wilderness moment, a journey that probably should have taken me a few years to accomplish has taken me 15 years to do. If you haven't figured it out by now, Confidential

Conversations™ is about transparency – about taking off the mask and being vulnerable enough to allow God to use you the way he needs to in order to build his kingdom. In 2001, I was laid off from what I knew at the time to be the best job a girl with no degree could have. Before the layoff, I had been promoted two times in less than a year, and the only administrative assistant traveling the country selling product and services all in the name of the company I worked, and making pretty good money too!

I eventually moved from the place I had called home in Atlanta, Georgia, to a place I called my wilderness. A place where the only person I knew was what I thought then to be a frenemy. You know her, she the chick you think is wearing your jersey, but she really isn't on your team. A person who I shared mutual friends with when she heard I was relocating to Baltimore, she offered me a bed to sleep in. A place where not only I needed her, but I found years later, she needed me too. It was in Baltimore when my entrepreneurial journey started. However, I didn't really know God's hands were on me. I would jokingly ask, what are you up too, but I never really attributed my success to Him! From 1999 to 2006 about 80% of the numbers in my phone were those of some of Hollywood's "A" list celebrities and the NFL's and NBA's highest paid professionals from coaches to athletes. During that time, I made some horrible decisions that like the children of Israel caused me to put "lifestyle" over God, and he humbled me.

Although God will give you up to the very thing you desire, He knows when we have been tried long enough. He knows how much we can stand and in our breaking process, the sifting and shifting that occurs, he knows not to break our spirits so he can't use us. Instead, he makes a new covenant with us and releases us on our journey to receive the promises he has made to us.

Even in our wilderness moments, God takes care of us until he is ready to move us to the next level. In our wilderness moments, he allows us to work to a certain level until he's ready to turn our pain into profit. Some of you reading today's conversation are in your wilderness right now, and God is taking care of you. You are able to buy food, pay your bills, have a car and a roof over your head, but he is saying, you have wandered long enough, it is time for you to turn and start a new journey.

The journey that will elevate you. The journey that will propel you. The journey that will cause you to be a blessing to others because now you are truly blessed. Ladies, your wilderness moment is your development period. It's the time that while he chastises you, he is also preparing you for restoration. This is the time where he humbles you and teaches you to put to shame the lustful thought and not just sexual and follow Him. To find comforts in him and what he can do. Some of you have been wandering for years. It's time to claim your promise land, to claim restoration and peace. It's time to be healed where you hurt, but you can't because what he showed you, you're afraid to claim it. It looks too big. It seems too hard. Your perception is skewed.

When you don't see yourself the way God sees you, you don't think you can do it. It was the same thing that happened to the children of Israel. In Deuteronomy 1:26, after Moses sent the spies to check out the land, 10 of 12 came back with reports that the city was filled with giants and even the buildings were too big, but what they failed to report was the city, and all they had seen was built on mounds. What they saw, while it appeared to be too big, was just a figment of their imagination.

They didn't see things the way God saw them! Like them, you don't' realize that God has already gone before you and checked out the camp. He knows what's there and what's not. He knows who you're going to have to fight and what weapons you're going to need. Ladies, who's in your camp? Who's not seeing things clearly? Who's in your camp with a skewed perception? Is it you? Are you seeing what God is going to do but because it looks too big you've turned your back on it?

Sistah, you've wandered long enough. It's time to recover. It's time to stand up and take your rightful place in the Kingdom. Don't let fear suffocate you and keep you from what God is releasing you to have, yet one more time. He's giving you a do-over.

UNVEIL THE MASK

Be strong and very courageous. Be careful to obey all the law my servant Moses gave you; do not turn from it to the right or to the left, that you may be successful wherever you go. Keep this Book of the Law always on your lips; meditate on it day and night, so that you may be careful to do everything written in it. Then you will be prosperous and successful. Have I not commanded you? Be strong and courageous. Do not be afraid; do not be discouraged, for the Lord your God will be with you wherever you go."

~Joshua 1:7-9 (NKJV)

Joshua and Caleb had the right idea. They had more confidence in God than in man. In order for them to possess God's promise to them, they had to wait until every man of fighting age died in the desert because of Israel's lack of faith. They were obedient without fault, not only to God but also to those in authority over them.

I encourage you to read Joshua 1. Joshua made it a practice to take God at His Word. So when God made him, Israel's leader after the death of Moses, He knew how He had processed Joshua to be ready to take His people into the promised land. It took 40 years, but He lived to see God's promise materialize and you will to if you hearken to the voice of the Lord.

DAY NINETEEN

How Bad Do You Want It?

ESPERATE TIMES CALL FOR DESPERATE measures. The question is how bad do you want it? When you begin to see things the way God sees them, your faith will be tested, and you will constantly find yourself asking, "is this all worth it?" The day that I got it when I realized He was processing me for purpose and after praying about it and crying my heart out, I had to stand up, fix my skirt, check my makeup and ask myself, "How Bad Do You Want It?" How bad do you want what God has for you?

Some of you reading today's conversation are probably asking yourself the same question and like you and I, Esther had to ask herself how bad did she want it? The Bible says she was an orphan and was left virtually to be a nonentity raised by her cousin Mordecai as his daughter with no particular promise in life until she was elevated to her place of purpose. As the story goes, Esther wasn't called by God, but she was used by Him. She was processed for purpose. God brings Esther on the scene to save a nation. She literally came out of nowhere and often that's how things work with us. God was looking for someone to fulfill his purpose, and he chose Esther and like Esther when he places you in a position to stand up, when it's your turn to get in the game, rise to the occasion to meet your destiny!

Ladies, you have to be willing to go through some things. You're going to have to be willing to fight a good fight and finish strong. God knew when he called you what you were going to have to deal with, but like Esther, he equipped you. In the story of Esther, her cousin-guardian Mordecai sends word back to saying, "For if you remain completely silent at this time, relief and deliverance will arise for the Jews from another place, but you and your father's house will perish. Yet who knew whether you have come to the kingdom for such as time as this!" In essence, what he was saying to Esther was, this is your season. This is not a time to be quiet. If you are quiet now, you may miss the real opportunity, purpose and reason for being right where God has placed you. When you begin to realize that God called you and you begin to see the big picture, while it's a beautiful thing, it will be a scary thing! But you can't be afraid to act under pressure. My mom used to tell us as kids, "A scary man can't win!" I didn't understand it then, but what she was telling us at the time was to try! So I say to you, a scary woman can't win! No matter how afraid you are, once you realize the resources you have at your disposal, once you realize the call on your life - - - what you were REALLY processed for, you have got to get out there and get it!

What are you afraid of? The King, the one who called you is there. You have gone through the training now it's time to put it to work! How do you do that though? By putting your agenda down. Putting aside any plans you think you have that will bring you notoriety. Stop holding on to the thing you're comfortable with. The thing that will give or have given you your perceived status quo. Put it down for a far greater purpose - Kingdom building! I read somewhere that truly effective women are those who can step away from their own short-sighted agendas to God's eternal purposes. Yeah, I know you thought the life you have, the car you drive, the house you live in or whatever great thing you may have accomplished was "it." But God said Sister, I put you on the scene for something far greater than the material possessions you were able to acquire. To fulfill my purpose. There is a plan much bigger and it is through you I want to accomplish it. When you realize why you are here, why you were processed for purpose and let your agenda become my agenda, we can do some things.

We know the familiar passage in Matthew 6:33, "But seek first the kingdom of God and all His righteousness, and all these things shall be added to you." So again, "How bad do you want it?" Are you willing to step down? Are you willing to risk it all? Are you willing to put your life on the line to save a nation like Esther? I know it's a hard pill to swallow, so let me see if I can give you a gel capsule. What did He give up for you? Who in your family is worth the risk? Who will you fight for? How bad do you want it? Esther had to ask herself the same questions, "How bad do I want it to save my people? Am I willing to step outside the palace courts without permission from my "husband-king" and risk death? Her answer was, Yes! And when she responded "yes," her obedience not only led her to saving herself and an entire nation, but God killed the one who set out to destroy her and the nation she risked it all to save. He also propelled her and her Uncle Mordecai to much bigger positions with greater responsibility. Now that you know you were processed for purpose, how bad do you want it because you're going to have to go through some stuff. It's not going to be easy, but with God I promise you, it will be well worth it!

UNVEIL THE MASK

Yes," Jesus replied, "and I assure you that everyone who has given up house or brothers or sisters or mother or father or children or property, for my sake and for the Good News, will receive now in return a hundred times as many houses, brothers, sisters, mothers, children, and property—along with persecution. And in the world to come that person will have eternal life. But many who are the greatest now will be least important then, and those who seem least important now will be the greatest then."

~Mark 10:29 -31 (NLT)

In this scripture, Jesus was answering an inquiry by one of His disciples about the cost of their serving Him. According to Mark 10:29 – 31, Christ's benefit plan supersedes any costs that we may incur as a result of our servitude to Him and building His kingdom. When you ask yourself what it costs to serve Christ, remember it cost Him everything to serve you and give you eternal life. In other words, God's benefits package will blow your mind!

DAY TWENTY

Pursuit to Recovery

RECOVERY IS DEFINED AS RETURNING TO YOUR normal state of mind or strength. To regain possession of or control of something stolen or lost, or to get back. When I look at what this word means I have mixed emotions. In one breath, I am mad at myself because of what I allowed the enemy to take from me, but in the same breath, I am just as excited because it says I am able to take back, to regain and to return to the place where God originally wanted me. However, sometimes getting back to that place where you were first purposed to be is not always as easy as it sounds, so in order to get there and to take back what was lost, you have to plan accordingly.

Listening in on a conference call with one of the youngest female millionaires in the world, Ms. Stormy Wellington, I heard her say, "Improper planning leads to piss poor performance." What a statement right? This statement will have you doing a bit of self-inspection to discover if or where you've not planned properly. Each of us is given 24 hours in a day. Not only is what you do in those 24 hours your gift back to God, but how you use your 24 hours will determine your success or failure in accomplishing the task at hand. So in your pursuit to recover, you have to stay hungry. Recovery doesn't get a day off. You have to work at it every day. You can't sleep all day or watch TV all day. You have to be willing to sacrifice. Eric Thomas, The Hip Hop Preacher says it best. He said, "It is not until your need to succeed is as bad as your need to breathe, will you succeed." Ladies, it is not until you realize that your recovery is a matter of life and death will you recover. You have to want restoration so bad that you can't sleep at night.

Stop worrying about what people say, you are the most important person in your recovery. Stop focusing on the old things, the things you have lost and start focusing on what you will gain if and when you change your mind. I'm not saying it will be easy, but I guarantee you, it will be worth it. Your recovery is going to require a lifestyle change. An alcoholic can't go to Alcoholic Anonymous and ween him or herself off of alcohol and continue to hang out with people who are drinking alcohol. Likewise, you are going to have to change your surroundings. Change where you frequent. Change what you feed your mind. What are you reading? What are you listening too? Who's in your clique that is still addicted to the old things you're trying to be delivered from? Romans 12:2 says, "Be not conformed of this world, but be ye transformed, which means to be made over by the renewing of your mind, that ye may prove what is that good, and acceptable, and perfect will of God." In your pursuit, you will need to transform and renew some things. It's going to take some renovating, and it is not going to happen overnight. It's not just going to happen miraculously! You are going to have to put in some work.

It is going to require mental toughness and you being deliberate in your actions and intentional in the way you think. You are going to have to get rid of the waste and clear the clutter. Whatever area of your life that you are clinging to, that's the area you need to release to God in your pursuit. You are going to have to prune some things, cut back and circumcise some things. It's like pruning a rose bush in the fall months. You need to get rid of the old, in preparation for the new thing God is doing in you.

UNVEIL THE MASK

This means that anyone who belongs to Christ has become a new person. The old life is gone; a new life has begun!

~2 Corinthians 5:17 (NLT)

One of the most beautiful times of the year is Spring. The flowers return and begin to bloom, and the birds start a liturgy at your windowsill. It makes your heart smile when you see the beauty of God's creation. It bears witness to God's plan of redemption for our lives. No matter how hard or harsh the Winter has been, Spring always shows up again. You can depend on God to make all things "new" in you because out of everything He has created, He created you alone in His image. Make a list of 10 things that remind you of the beauty of God in your life. You will be surprised how He has already started the process of restoring righteousness to your life. He was simply waiting for you to say "yes," so that He could reveal His divine plan to reveal the beauty He placed inside of you. Bloom my sister, bloom.

DAY TWENTY-ONE

Lest You Forget

C AN YOU BELIEVE IT? WE ARE ON DAY 21 OF the devotional and boy has it been a journey. As I write today's entry, I'm reminded of the pain and triumph I've endured the past 20 months; and how God has changed me each step of the way. In my study time preparing for The Conversation, my weekly live broadcast on Periscope, the Holy Spirit stopped me at Deuteronomy 1, verses 6-7, saying, "You have dwelt long enough at this mountain, turn and take your journey..." I didn't understand it at first, so I kept reading, but as the Lord would have it, I couldn't rest until I started to see things the way he saw them. And then I had an epiphany! I got it! He was releasing me. I was getting a do-over, a chance to move forward again. My time in the wilderness was ending, and he was telling me to take up my bed and walk!

How amazing is that? When God knows that you now see things the way he sees them and him in his awesomeness says, it's time for your blessing. I told you in an earlier chapter that the breaking process is brutal and that it will last as long as it has too until you start to see things the way he sees them. I also told you that during the breaking process, the one thing God wouldn't do is break you in such a way that the purpose for your life couldn't be fulfilled. Ladies, isn't that good news? That he loves us so much that despite our wretchedness, and our ugly messed up selves he will not leave us in the state that he found us! But as I close, here's what I want you to remember. In his releasing you and giving you a second or for some a third or fourth chance, lest you forget, the one who gave you the power to start over. The one who gave you the power to get wealth. Lest you forget ladies, how you got there. Deuteronomy 6, verses 10-12, says, when (that's a promise there), He gives you your promise land that he swore to Abraham, Isaac and Jacob to give you cities you did not build, house filled with good things, which you did not fill, vineyards and olive trees you did not plant and when you have eaten and are full, do not forget Him!

Don't forget the Lord who brought you out! That it is not me, La Tanya, or you reading who did it for yourself and start chasing the lifestyle, the limelight, cliques, cars and clothes and all the material things his restoring you brought. I'm not saying you are not supposed to enjoy them, but do not forget what you had to be delivered from to get it! Do not forget the development period, your wilderness where you wandered for years until you decided to be obedient. Don't forget where it took you years to figure out what could have taken you days to do. Or when he showed you, you and he let you go hungry, then fed you manna to show you that you could live by bread alone to humble you. Where he wrestled with you like Jacob to test you! To test your stamina and your will to see IF you were strong enough – determined enough! To see if you would really ride or die and would do whatever it was to get to what HE was giving you!!

Listen when the blessings start to flow and they will flow, lest you forget that in your wilderness your clothes and shoes didn't wear out. That means they still fit, they were still in style until he was ready to change the style...sister, they still looked good!!! That in your wilderness, during your development period he chastised you so that this day, the day that he delivered and started to restore you, that you would fear him! That you would walk how he says to walk, say what he tells you to say and move how and when HE SAYS MOVE!!!

Ladies, this is the season you're coming out! The promise is still in effect, but as he brings you out - when he brings you out remember him! Remember it was he, who gave you the power to get wealth! Remember he was the one who fed you when you were hungry. Made you the head and not the tale – the lender and not the borrower.

The Word of God goes on to say that you are a chosen people and that before he knew you and he chose you! That he set you apart to be prophets to great nations. Sister, we have jobs to do, and it is through the things you will receive in your promise land that you will be able to do those things! His saving you is not just about you, nor his delivering and prospering you is about you. It is about Kingdom building! So, lest you forget because if you forget, the Bible reassures us of the consequences of our sin.

I don't know about you, but the past 20 months have been taxing on me, and while I've grown tremendously, there is absolutely no way, I will forget where he's brought me from. No way I will take the credit for something I couldn't have done if not for him. Ladies, some of you have been wandering for years. Your tear ministry required flood insurance, you've labored, and this is your season of breakthrough! As much as you wrestled in your wilderness, some of you limping to the finish line to conquer what the Lord has shown you, don't you dare forget him when he gives it to you.

UNVEIL THE MASK AND REMEMBER

I will remember the deeds of the LORD; yes, I will remember your miracles of long ago.

~Psalms 77:11 (NIV)

Ladies, I salute you for completing this journey. I know God is pleased with your progress, and I expect that I will hear quite a few testimonies as a result. God has brought us a mighty long way, and I would like to encourage you to set aside a time to thank Him for what He has done, is doing, and will do in the future. Weekly, monthly, quarterly, semiannually or annually; whatever timeframe you chose to do it in, I recommend that you consistently show God an attitude of gratitude for the mighty work He has done in us. He is a GOOD, GOOD, GOD!

Acknowledgements

FRANCES L. ROPER. I GUESS I CAN FINALLY SAY I did it! I sat down long enough to "focus." Momma, I am the woman I am today because of you. The strength and tenacity I have; I get from you. My wit and crazy sense of humor, I got that from you too! Lady, you are spewed all over this book from crazy anecdotes and funny sayings to my standing firm and picking myself up by my bootstraps (oh yeah, I finally figured out what bootstraps were. I actually looked them up for this one) to keep moving forward. I know I work every one of your nerves with this entrepreneurial "thing" and being consumed all the time on "that" Internet. I even know that sometimes if not all of the time it doesn't make sense to you, but I promise you, God is doing something really special in my life that you and He will smile on. I love you to life!

TEMPESTT BRE'ELLE. 'Girrl', as you so lovingly call me couldn't have done any of this without you. This past year has been tough, but your strength through it all has been phenomenal. You have poured into me in more ways than you can ever begin to imagine and I thank God for the woman you're becoming! These past few months have brought us closer together as mom and daughter. I didn't understand why at first, but as time passed God showed me. You are well on your way. Keep trusting in Him for all things and he will give you the desires of your heart.

TO MY BROTHER, SISTER'S, BROTHER-IN-LAW, AND NEPHEW. Andre' Roper, Fred & Kimberly Green, Coretta Mallet-Fontenot and Jahmail Thomas, who support me more than I truly deserve and put up with me even more. I love you.

TO MY FAVORITE AUNT CHARLOTTE, AND THE ENTIRE Roper clan who loves me for just being me. I love you more!

DR. REMUS E. WRIGHT, well sir, since this is my book, I guess I can be partial when I say, "You are the absolute best shepherd in the world, and I am honored to serve under your leadership and call The Fountain of Praise home." You have taught and I have learned so much about leading in excellence, serving with humility and being obedient to the voice of God. Thank you for your obedience and showing me as long as I am obedient to the voice of God, there is no limit to where he'll take me. I pray God's continued blessings on you, WrightPath Ministries and all that you do. Love you P!

FIRST LADY MIA K. WRIGHT. It's been said that you never know who's watching until you hear what you've done right or wrong in the eyes of another. Lady Mia, let me be one of those who's publicly saying, "you've got it right!" You have been silently mentoring me for the past two years and I have learned a lot. You are a woman of such style and grace, and I can only pray to grow into the Woman of God you are. In your transparency, you have shown me that it's okay to unveil my mask, walk in my purpose and live my change no matter what. I love you beautiful butterfly! Keep shining, because they are watching.

DR. CONNIE STEWART. Words cannot express my gratitude. Not just for the support of this book, but for me. When I met you, you saw through me, yet you didn't pass judgment. You simply 'coached' me and reassured me that where I was, was the place right where God wanted me. You encouraged me to take what I already had and to simply bloom where He planted me. Thank you! #Bloomnation

SHARON C. JENKINS. We all have heard the saying, "I'm pregnant with purpose." That was me, pregnant with purpose in need of a midwife to coach, support and provide expertise that would help me deliver my book baby. And then I met you. Girlfriend your skills are simply impeccable. Thank you your support and for giving my words life! I can't wait to collaborate on the next one!

TO THE BEST GROUP OF CHICKS, A GIRL COULD EVER ASK FOR, Edrea Aldridge, Joi Beasley, Mechelle Graham-Brown, Yulonda Buster, Dee Cleare, Layle McKelvey, Twiler Portis, Kalena Tyus, Mia McPeters-Spicer, Cynthia Griffin-White and Adriane Williams, thank you for your undying support. You cried with me and allowed me to cry without judgment. You remained constant even when the phone stopped ringing. You prayed with me and for me; and most importantly you encouraged to simply share my story. I love you all.

SHIWANA L. REED. My sister, my friend. Chile, I have complained for almost a decade to you about not answering your phone when I call or when you do, how you'd be so busy you'd rush me to get off. But thank God for the day you did answer and didn't rush. We laughed, cried and eventually ended the call with you telling me that I was the Olivia Pope of small business, that if anyone could fix it, I could. While God had other plans for me and my business, those words reignited me and caused me to seek him more. Oh, how grateful I am that you answered. Love you girl!

TO MY CHURCH FAMILY AT THE FOUNTAIN OF PRAISE, with special thanks and appreciation to Elder Reva Witherspoon, Wilson Tucker, Minister Shirley Tucker, Dr. Sabrina Echols-Sampson, Reverend Yolanda Burroughs, Reverend Arthur Rucker, Minister Steffanie Bernstein, Evangelist Bridgette Ross-Daniels, Minister Helen Patterson, Minister Regina Perkins,

Minister Regina Kelly, Evangelist Lisa Ricardo, Minister RoLonda Brown, Minister Ardrienne Bradberry, Minister Dorthea Davis and The Calling Ministry, FLOURISH Ministry, my MDAC 2015-2016 class, Pamela Britton, Yvette Goree and Kimberly Nelson, thank you for standing in the gap. Be it a ride, kind words, your prayers, encouragement to write, and even financial blessings when God saw fit, I will always be indebted to you.

MY BROTHER'S KEEPER'S. Council Member Dwight Boykins, Dr. Christopher Edwards, Delano, Willliam Lomax and David Boone, thank you for your guidance, advice and brotherly push when I needed most.

KEVIN LODER, my man! Who knew when I met six-six almost 2 years ago to talk shop that you'd be the small forward God would use to play point and drive the ball when I needed it most. You are one of the coolest and smartest brothers I know. In case I hadn't told you, I see that thang the way He sees it now, and you guessed it, it was in me all along! I love you man and thank God for our meeting. Thank you! Thank you! Thank you!

THE "ERWIN W. PORTIS". Words cannot express the love and gratitude I have for you. Although our time together was short-lived, there was not one day I didn't learn something from you. As I reflect on how you "forced" me to help you publish your book, "Enriching The Total You: You Are The Answer", I know now it was God's design to position and prepare me to publish my own. So I guess I can say, I got the F&D (focus and discipline) part down long enough to finish, this time what I started. I'm going to miss you my dear Coach and Mentor, but in your memory I promise to do my best to #LiveFull and #DieEmpty. Rest in Heaven.

MICHAEL A. WASHINGTON, my voice of reason. I purposely saved you for last. Words cannot express how grateful I am to have you in my life. From the day I met you, I knew God had something special planned for us, I just didn't know that it would be of such magnitude. You didn't know it at the time, but I was at the lowest point of my life and was terribly broken when we met. It was your strength and love for God that allowed me to take off the first of many masks I wore. Even when I tried to run (and that was quite a few times), you'd find the right words that always led to God's words to make me sit still. When I look at you and recall all that you have endured, you show me that despite what it looks like, God is still God and controls it all. Watching you come back, not one time, but twice after being told it couldn't be done taught me to trust God, even when it didn't make sense. I know half the time you thought I wasn't listening, or half-way paying attention, but I heard you loud and clear. Thank you for being my friend first and not cutting me any slack, because you knew what cloth I was cut from, but most importantly thank you for being you. Love you!

About The Author

L A TANYA D. WALKER IS AN ORDINARY GIRL, WITH AN extraordinary story of faith, perseverance and triumph. A story she often shares through motivational speaking, preached Word, and her weekly live broadcast on Periscope. La Tanya is a serialpreneur having owned either solely or through partnership, five successful businesses from Houston to Atlanta. Her entrepreneurial career spans over 15 years and has afforded her phenomenal opportunities that assisted thousands of aspiring entrepreneurs and high net-worth individuals to start, manage and operate successful for-profit and non-profit businesses.

As an accomplished business owner, La Tanya has received numerous awards and recognition for her outstanding business success, to include the Greater Houston Black Chamber of Commerce, Mack H. Hannah, Jr. Upstart Award Recipient and Pinnacle Awards Finalist, Who's Who in Black Atlanta and Houston. La Tanya's vision is clear: to empower, restore and transform the lives of broken women enabling them to live life on purpose through Confidential Conversations™ Women's Empowerment Network, a national women's organization located in Houston, Texas and by Də'zīneU, a professional development and virtual university that provides workshops, executive roundtables, coaching and mastermind sessions for aspiring and small woman business owners and entrepreneurs.

La Tanya's platform includes women's conferences, workshops, non-profit organizations, coaching seminars, Chambers of Commerce, church groups, corporations and women business owners.

About Confidential Conversations™

WHAT STARTED OUT AS A PERSONAL JOURNEY TO ME resulted in a God-size vision and La Tanya's life's purpose to restore the brokenhearted and empower women across the country to live in true authenticity. Confidential Conversations™, Women's Empowerment Network, Inc., is a non-profit organization seeking its 501 (c)3 status with programming to support the total woman.

Programs and services include – The Conversation, an Internet broadcast that streams live weekly,

Confidential Conversations™ Real Talk with Real Women Power Luncheon, Authentically You!™ Women's Retreat, and byDə'zīneU™, a leadership institute for women in business. Through this unique blend of programs, services and ministry outreach, women globally can expect their lives to be enriched.